New York City
HISTRY
for Kids

From New Amsterdam to the Big Apple

— WITH 21 ACTIVITIES —

Richard Panchyk

CHICAGO
REVIEW
PRESS

© 2012 by Richard Panchyk

Published by Chicago Review Press, Incorporated

814 North Franklin Street

Chicago, Illinois 60610

ISBN 978-1-883052-93-5

Library of Congress Cataloging-in-Publication Data

Panchyk, Richard.

    New York City history for kids : from New Amsterdam to the Big Apple, with 21 activities / Richard Panchyk.

    p. cm.

    Includes bibliographical references and index.

    ISBN 978-1-883052-93-5

    1. New York (N.Y.)—History—Study and teaching (Primary)—Activity programs.

    I. Title.

    F128.29.P36 2012

    372.89—dc23

                                    2012029893

Cover and interior design: Monica Baziuk

Cover images: (front, clockwise from upper right) Empire State Building, Christopher Penler/Shutterstock.com; Statue of Liberty, courtesy of the Carol M. Highsmith Archive, Library of Congress, Prints and Photographs Division; Chrysler Building, nadirco/Shutterstock.com; Brooklyn Bridge, courtesy of the Library of Congress (LOC); Cyclone roller coaster in Coney Island, Elliotte Rusty Harold/Shutterstock.com; Jackie Robinson, LOC; sledding in Central Park, c. 1915, LOC; bagel, RusGri/Shutterstock.com; (back, clockwise from upper right) Woolworth Building, c. 1912, LOC; St. Patrick's Cathedral, author's collection; street vendors, 1910, LOC; Peter Stuyvesant, LOC; lion sculpture at New York Public Library, LOC; New York in 1736, LOC

Interior images: Courtesy of the Library of Congress: pp. ii, v, viii, 1, 5, 10 (right), 11, 16, 18, 20–21, 26, 30–31, 32, 35, 37, 41, 42, 44, 47 (top), 48–49, 52, 54, 59, 66, 67, 69, 72, 76, 78, 79, 80, 81, 82, 83, 84, 86, 88 (left), 89, 90, 93 (right), 99, 100–101, 102, 105, 109, 111, 116, 117, 119, 122, 128, 131; courtesy of the U.S. Geological Survey: p. 2; Mark Baziuk: pp. 6, 27, 40 (left), 94, 115, 120; all other images from the author's collection

5 4 3 2 1

The Flip Flap roller coaster in Coney Island, Brooklyn, circa 1900.

For Carl, Maria, Herman, and Sophia

Contents

Acknowledgments

So MANY PEOPLE have fostered my love for New York City over the years. Thanks to my Stuyvesant High School teacher Philip Scandura for his fascinating class on the history of New York. Thanks to my editor, Jerome Pohlen, and the folks at Chicago Review Press for proposing this topic. A special thanks to my family and my friends for supporting and encouraging me. And thanks to you, New York City! Love ya!

NOVUM AMSTERODAMUM

Time Line

1600s

1700s

1900s

1807	Robert Fulton's steamship departs from Manhattan to Albany
1808	Collect Pond filled
1811	Randel "grid plan" developed for the layout of NYC streets
1825	Erie Canal is completed
1827	Delmonico's opens
1832	Cholera kills over 3,500 people
1835	Great fire
1841	Barnum's American Museum opens
1842	Croton water system is completed
1849	Astor Place Riot
1853	World Exhibition is held at the newly built Crystal Palace
1857–64	Central Park is constructed
1863	Draft Riots
1871	William "Boss" Tweed is arrested
1882	First electric lights in the city
1883	Brooklyn Bridge opens
1886	Statue of Liberty is completed
1888	Blizzard cripples the city
1892	Ellis Island opens
1898	Consolidation Act takes effect, combining Brooklyn, Queens, Staten Island, and Bronx with Manhattan

1902	Macy's opens in Herald Square
1904	NYC subway opens; *General Slocum* fire
1911	Triangle Shirtwaist fire
1919	Prohibition begins
1920	Babe Ruth joins the Yankees
1929	Stock market crash
1931	Empire State Building is completed
1939–40	World's Fair is held at Flushing Meadows, Queens
1950	First part of the United Nations complex opens
1963	Old Penn Station is demolished
1964	Beatles arrive in New York
1964–65	World's Fair is held at Flushing Meadows, Queens
1977	Blackout plunges the city into darkness; massive looting follows
1986	Javits Convention Center opens
2001	Twin Towers are destroyed in terrorist attack
2012	Freedom Tower becomes tallest building in the city

1800s

Introduction

I OFTEN TRY TO imagine what life was like for my great-great-grandfather, Carl Friedrich. He was the first of my ancestors to arrive in New York City. When he set foot on Manhattan Island in 1866 as a young man of 18, what a sight must have greeted his eyes. What a commotion! People everywhere were bustling about. There were endless streets lined with imposing stone buildings. What a clatter must have greeted his ears—the clicking of horse hooves on the pavement, the cries of street hawkers, the shrill whistle of policemen, and the rumbling of streetcars, stagecoaches, and carriages. No longer was young Carl in his little German hometown of 8,000. He was alone in a teeming city of well over a million inhabitants.

It was noisy and crowded. Some people in rags, others in top hats and sporting fancy walking sticks. People of all kinds, everywhere!

Carl had little money. He had to take whatever job he could find, and he lived in a filthy, cramped tenement on the Lower East Side. This was the only lodging he could afford. There was one bathroom that he shared with the others on his floor, and it was wretched. There were bugs and mice everywhere.

Carl worked hard. After a few years he became a US citizen, moved uptown to a better neighborhood, found a wife, and started his own pickle business. Before long his own delivery trucks were adding to the clatter of the city as they drove to saloons, delivering his condiments. He was now joining in the same clatter that may have shocked his ears at first, the clatter of commerce, the noise of a thriving metropolis. His own children were adding to the commotion, running around and playing on 78th Street. Life wasn't easy. Carl could have given up and returned to Germany. But he stayed put and made it work.

In a way, it's through Carl's determination that I'm here, writing this book. Carl and millions of others like him are the people who have made New York great. This is Carl's story. This is all of their stories. The story of New York. I hope that you enjoy it.

Mannahatta

THE FIRST VISITORS to what is now New York City were glaciers. During the last ice age, a 1,000-foot-thick sheet of ice crept down from Canada and covered half of the future city. The Wisconsin Ice Sheet reached New York about 20,000 years ago and then stopped, creating a ridge running through Brooklyn and Queens called the *terminal moraine*.

The ice made a big impact on the terrain of New York, depositing boulders, polished pebbles, and sand that had been carried along by the ice as it advanced from the north. After a couple thousand years, a warm-up began, and the ice started to retreat (melt), completely vanishing between about 12,000 and 13,000 years ago.

The lines on this rock in Bronx Park were made by debris dragged across it by a visiting glacier during the ice age.

After the area thawed, Manhattan Island was a hilly, forested land rich with wildlife, including bears, beavers, deer, panthers, wolves, and over 200 species of birds. There were forests that were home to dozens of different kinds of trees and countless varieties of plants. There were fish-filled ponds and creeks and streams. Manhattan was a lush paradise, a greatly diverse land, from its rocky northern reaches to the swamps of the southern portion.

Native Americans

OVER 10,000 years ago, the first Native Americans began to settle on the 13-mile-long island they came to call Mannahatta (which means "island of many hills") and the surrounding area. These natives belonged to the Lenape (or Delawaran) tribe, part of the Algonquin nation.

There were three different groups living in small settlements concentrated in different parts of the island: in lower Manhattan, the Manahate; in upper-middle Manhattan, the Rechgawawank; and at the very northern reaches of the island, the Wickquasgeck. There were also the Canarsies in Brooklyn and the Matinecocks in Queens, among others. Relatively few details are known about the history of these natives before European contact.

The Lenape used body paint to make colorful markings on their faces, arms, legs, and chests. They wore embroidered, tanned animal skins for clothing and used feathers for decoration. They lived in single-family wigwams and multifamily longhouses. They planted corn, beans, and squash, and cultivated chestnuts and hazelnuts. The Lenape also hunted animals such as deer using bows and arrows. They caught plenty of fish (especially striped bass) using large nets and dined regularly on oysters; their discarded piles of shells lined the waterfront in lower Manhattan. They used tools made of wood, bone, and stone. For money they used *wampum*—small beads made of clam and periwinkle shells.

The natives of Manhattan used one main north/south trail to get from one end of the island to the other, what we call the Wickquasgeck Road today. This trail ran along present-day Broadway at the southern tip of Manhattan and remained east of what is now Fifth Avenue until about 86th Street, then went north-northwest, passing through Central Park and then passing the eastern edge of what is now Fort Tryon Park.

After millennia of living in the area, everything would change fairly quickly for these first New Yorkers. The world as they knew it would soon vanish once strangely dressed, pale-faced explorers began to arrive in their huge ships.

Europeans Arrive

SAILING ON behalf of France in 1524, the Italian explorer Giovanni da Verrazano (1485–1528) was the first European to arrive in New York harbor. He found natives dressed in colorful feathers who "came towards us with evident delight, raising shouts of admiration, and showing us where we could most securely land our boat." In 1525, Esteban Gomez, a Portuguese explorer sailing for Spain, visited the area and brought back furs and Native American slaves.

Henry Hudson (c. 1570–1611), an Englishman, was hired by the newly formed Dutch East India Company to locate the elusive "Northwest Passage" to China, which would allow ships to avoid the long and difficult trip around the southern tip of Africa. Hudson set sail in 1607 and again in 1608, but both times he had to turn back before getting too far. In 1609, Hudson and a crew of 18 tried again, but they failed to discover such a passage in the icy waters to the north. The crew forced him to abandon his northern track and steer southwest, and thus they reached New York harbor.

The Manhattan Indians were friendly at first, and they paddled their canoes out to the *Half Moon* to trade their furs for some trinkets. Robert Juet, Hudson's first mate, recorded the events of September 13:

Henry Hudson.

We turned into the river two leagues and anchored. This morning . . . there came eight and twentie canoes full of men, women and children to betray us; but we saw their intent, and suffered none of them to come aboord of us. At twelve of the clocke they departed. They brought with them oysters and beanes, whereof wee bought some.

Hudson himself wrote of Manhattan, "It is as beautiful a land as one can tread upon . . .

The discovery of the Hudson River, 1609.

Make Samp Porridge

WHEN THE settlers came to the New World, many of the foods from their homelands were not available. To eat, they took their cues from the Native Americans, who not only had corn as a staple of their diet but also had become experts at breeding hybrids of different corn varieties, partly to get the most out of every growing season.

One word for corn was "samp," and the Native Americans made samp porridge from ground dried corn, water, and beans. It was a slow-simmering dish, and the settlers found they could make the base of cornmeal (hominy grits) and water, and then let it simmer in a big kettle in the hearth all week, each day adding ingredients to form that evening's meal. Depending on what foods were readily available, the porridge could vary from day to day. Besides beans, other items that were added to the hominy included root vegetables such as potatoes, carrots, parsnips, turnips, and onions. Salt pork, corned beef, and even shellfish might complete the meal. By the end of the week, there was an outer crust on the porridge, which tasted like popcorn.

The Dutch settlers who came to what is now New York modified the samp porridge to resemble a traditional dish from Holland, called "hutespot." Try the Dutch recipe below. If you like, make it again and use some of the other ingredient ideas.

Adult supervision required

What You Need
+ 2 cups hominy grits
+ 1 pound corned beef
+ 1 pound potatoes, peeled and cut into 1-inch chunks
+ 1 pound carrots, peeled and cut into 1-inch chunks
+ 1 medium turnip, peeled and cut into 1-inch chunks
+ 1 tablespoon chopped fresh herbs, such as parsley
+ salt and pepper

Place grits and meat in a large pot and add 1 gallon of water. Bring to a boil. Lower heat, cover, and simmer for three hours. Add vegetables to the pot; simmer 30 minutes or until tender. Add herbs and salt and pepper to taste.

and abounds in all kinds of excellent timber for building ships and for making large casks."

The next day, however, one of Hudson's crewmen, John Coleman, was killed by an arrow after a small party of men had gone ashore to explore. Hudson decided to sail on and saw great promise in the river that now bears his name. It was wide and deep, and he thought it could possibly lead to the Pacific Ocean. The *Half Moon* sailed upriver, and things still looked promising. He had reached the area of Haverstraw, where the river is more than three miles wide, and was encouraged. But soon after, the river narrowed. By the time he reached what is now Albany on September 19, Hudson saw that the river was no longer navigable. Still, he sent a crew in a small boat further upriver, but they found the water was only seven feet deep there. He began his return trip down the river on September 23.

Native Americans boarded the *Half Moon* at its stops along the way, but one native was killed sneaking about the cabin, and another was killed in the chaos that ensued. At Manhattan Island, two canoes of natives approached the vessel and began to fire arrows. The crew raised their muskets and aimed at the attackers, killing several of them. By October 4, Hudson's crew forced Hudson to set course for European soil. The hostilities during Hudson's voyage left 1 of the crew and 11 Native Americans dead.

The Dutch were eager to stake a claim in the New World, as the English and French had already done.

The *Onrust* was the first ship built
by Europeans in New York.

After a disappointed Hudson filed his report on the voyage with the Dutch East India Company, another ship returned to the New York Bay the following year, 1610, carrying goods to trade with the Native Americans and a crew that consisted of some of Hudson's men.

The next to make the trip was Dutch explorer and trader Adriaen Block (c. 1567–1627). On his second voyage to the New World in 1614, Block's ship *De Tijger* ("the Tiger") was anchored off the southern tip of Manhattan when a fire broke out. As the story goes, Block and his crew swam to shore and the ship burned to the waterline; there was nothing they could do to save her. They were stranded; with winter approaching, they had no choice but to wait out the cold weather. With the aid of the Native Americans, Block and his men constructed four makeshift log houses and became the first Europeans to live in what is now New York City.

The crew built a 42-foot-long, 16-ton replacement boat named the *Onrust* ("the Wanderer"). Though it was a worthy craft, Block deemed this boat too small for the ocean crossing. Nonetheless, he did use it to further explore the area. It was Block who bestowed the name "Hell Gate" upon a treacherously rocky stretch of water in the upper East River (the future scene of numerous shipwrecks). He ventured 60 miles up the Connecticut River and also discovered and named Block Island off the coast of Rhode Island. While sailing near Cape Cod, he made contact with another Dutch ship, left the *Onrust* behind, and returned to Holland. Though he was granted exclusive three-year trading rights in the New York area, he never returned to the New World.

By this time, Spanish posts had already been established in the South and Southwest, French posts in the St. Lawrence River Valley, and an English settlement at Jamestown. Sending ships to the New World was no longer about finding a shortcut to China and the Spice Islands. Now it was simply a race to claim the remaining land along the East Coast. The Dutch recognized that if they were to have a piece of North America, they had to act fast. In fact, the Pilgrims had originally intended to land at the mouth of the Hudson River in 1620 but decided to remain at Plymouth instead.

NEW NETHERLAND

From the Map of

A. VANDERDONCK

1656.

New Amsterdam

I N 1621, A new fur-trading company was formed, aimed at establishing a permanent settlement in the New World. The Dutch West India Company advertised for colonists, and the first ship of settlers arrived in May 1624 just in the nick of time; a French ship was about to claim the land for France based on Giovanni da Verrazano's voyage. The Dutch ship *New Netherland*, armed with two cannons, scared away the French ship.

Though 30 families had sailed from Holland on Captain Cornelius May's *New Netherland* on March 31, 1624, only eight families were to remain in the New York area, on Nut Island (now Governor's Island). Others would disembark at Fort Orange (now Albany), Fort Nassau (now Gloucester,

❮ Map of New Netherland in 1656.

New Jersey), and along the Connecticut River near present-day Hartford. In 1625 the company sent three more ships, loaded with horses, cattle, farming implements, and seed; several additional families; a governor, William Verhulst; and a surveyor and engineer, Cryn Fredericks. The southern tip of Manhattan Island was selected for the settlement. With that, the original eight families moved to Manhattan and the village of New Amsterdam was begun. The company also began clearing land to the north for use as *bouweries* (farms). The Dutch traders found the region to be rich with raw materials, especially furs, that could be exported to Holland for profit.

The Best Real Estate Deal Ever?

In December 1625, Peter Minuit (1580–1638) was selected to be governor of New Netherland, and he arrived at New Amsterdam the following spring. In May 1626, he set up a meeting with some of the local Native American leaders and purchased Manhattan Island for 60 guilders worth of trinkets, including beads, knives, and cloth. A 19th-century writer calculated this to be the equivalent of 24 dollars, but the natives probably did not think they were selling the land, only allowing the Dutch to share it with them.

As word spread of the profitable fur trade, the small settlement grew. The colonists planted crops such as wheat, rye, barley, oats, buckwheat, beans, and flax. By the end of 1626, colonists had already exported more than 7,000 beaver skins to Europe, along with nearly 1,000 otter, mink, and wildcat skins. Minuit oversaw the construction of about 30 small homes and Fort Amsterdam at the southern tip of the island.

The settlers were muddling along. Jonas Michaelius, New Amsterdam's first minister,

Minuit (seated) purchases Manhattan from the Native Americans, 1626.

wrote in 1628 that the settlement "lack[s] about 10 or 12 farmers with horses, cows, and sufficient laborers to supply us with bread, milk, and other necessities." Machinery for building sawmills was brought from Holland, and one was constructed on Governor's Island.

By 1628, there were about 270 people in New Amsterdam. Though New Netherland was doing okay, its profit was nothing compared to other ventures. Most of the Dutch West India Company's income was expected to come from war. The capture of Pernambuco (Brazil) in 1630 was a great victory for the Dutch. Admiral Peter Heyn sailed back to Holland with 17 ships loaded with Spanish treasure worth 12–14 million guilders. The trade in the whole of New Netherland was only 50,000 guilders per year. The Dutch West India Company wanted New Netherland to thrive, so in 1629, it issued a proclamation announcing the start of the *patroonship* system, whereby anyone desiring land in New Netherland (except Manhattan) would be given it providing he brought 50 colonists to settle the land shortly thereafter.

By the time Minuit was dismissed in 1632 over an investigation into possible misuse of company funds, New Amsterdam had a population of more than 300 and had sent more than 50,000 animal furs back to Europe. Though at first the company tightly controlled all land,

it eventually eased the restrictions to attract more colonists.

Melting Pot

NEW AMSTERDAM was a melting pot from the beginning. The first settlers were actually not "Dutch" but French-speaking Walloons from Holland and Huguenots from France seeking a better life. There were also some English settlers in the colony. Between 1648 and 1658, public documents in New Amsterdam were issued in French in addition to Dutch and English. There were also Africans (slaves), Jews, and representatives from many other cultures in the young city.

In 1646, a missionary named Isaac Jogues wrote, "On the Island of Manhatte, and in its environs, there may well be four or five hundred men of different sects and nations; the Director-General told me that there were men of eighteen different languages."

Kieft's War

A 1639 law forbade the sale of guns, powder, and lead to the Native Americans "on pain of being punished by Death," but the settlers did it anyway. Twenty beaver skins for one gun was

Wouter Van Twiller was director-general of New Netherland from 1633 to 1638.

Build a Replica of Fort Amsterdam/Fort George

THE FIRST Dutch settlers were concerned about attack by both Native Americans and the British. The small earthen fort, built while Peter Minuit was governor, offered a wide view of the harbor and the East and Hudson Rivers. Minuit's successor, Wouter Van Twiller, had a windmill added to the southwest corner of the fort to grind the grain necessary to feed the soldiers housed there. But Van Twiller did little to improve the fort, and when the next governor, Willem Kieft, arrived in 1638, he noted that the fort was "open on every side, so that nothing could obstruct going in or coming out, except at the stone point."

Inside the fort were several government buildings, including the governor's home, housing for soldiers, and a church (built in 1642). However, the fort was not too secure. Pigs dug holes in the earthen fort walls, and stones used to strengthen the walls were carried off by dishonest settlers. An observer wrote in 1650, "The fort under which we shelter ourselves, and from which as it seems all authority proceeds, lies like a mole heap or a tottering wall, on which there is not one gun carriage or one piece of cannon in a suitable frame or on a good platform."

In this activity, you will make a model of the fort.

What You Need

- 10 pounds of modeling clay
- Flat base, about 2 feet by 2 feet (foam core, cardboard, or poster board)
- Butter knife or similar smoothing tool
- Box of toothpicks

Study the image on the right, which shows the fort (mostly unchanged from Dutch times) in 1776. Plan to make your fort about 6 inches on each side and 3 inches high. Divide your clay into eight pieces, four for the walls and four for the bastions (corners). Use the knife to smooth and shape the bastion pieces and to smooth the joints when attaching the pieces to each other.

Governor's house and church, as they would have appeared in the 1640s.

Now place a toothpick into each bastion to represent guns. If you have leftover clay, fashion a governor's house, soldiers' barracks, and a church to go inside the fort, and maybe a few homes clustered outside the fort.

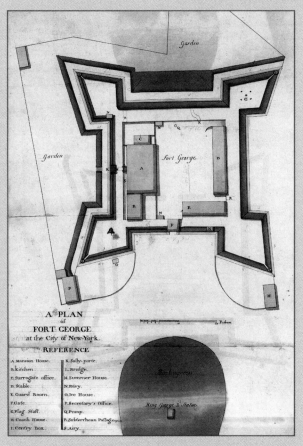

The fort, as it appeared in 1776.

quite profitable. Meanwhile, Governor Willem Kieft was looking for a reason to start trouble. He sent 100 men to Staten Island to take revenge on the Raritan Indians for allegedly stealing some pigs. The Dutch killed several natives. In reply, the Raritans burned down a Dutch farmhouse and killed four people.

Then, in 1641, a Wickquasgeck Indian showed up at the door of a wheelwright named Claes Smit who lived a few miles north of New Amsterdam. The native claimed to be interested in buying some cloth but then killed Smit when his back was turned, in revenge for the murder of his uncle 15 years before. Kieft demanded that the man's tribe produce the killer and hand him over at once. The Native Americans refused to comply.

In August 1641, Kieft called all heads of families to a meeting, and 12 men were chosen to serve on a special council to deal with the native situation. The council, led by David De Vries (who lived across the Hudson in what is now New Jersey), was to decide whether the Dutch should take revenge on Smit's murderer if the Native Americans did not surrender him. Should their whole village be destroyed? How, when, and by whom should the deed be done?

Though Kieft was eager for war, the citizens of New Amsterdam were not. The council said that force should be used only if necessary. Kieft

was not pleased with their report. He thanked them for their service but forbade the 12 from meeting again, under threat of punishment.

Early in 1643, a Native American killed a Dutchman who was roofing a house in Pavonia (New Jersey). Shortly after, two groups of Wickquasgeck Indians came to the New Amsterdam area seeking refuge from the hostile Mohawk Indians. One group settled at Corlear's Hook in Manhattan, just south of where

Map of Manhattan Island and surrounding area, 1639.

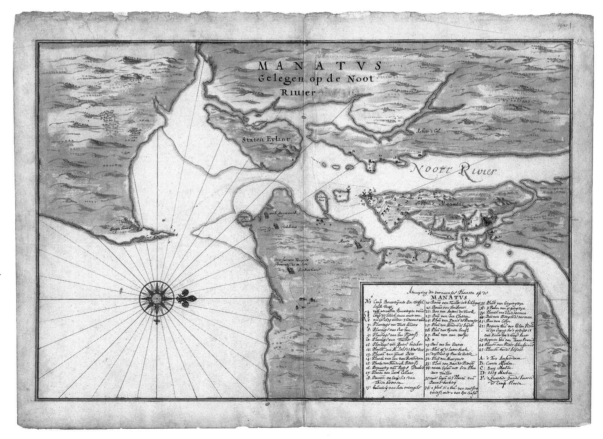

the Williamsburg Bridge stands today. The other, larger group was across the Hudson River at Pavonia.

This was just the opportunity Kieft sought. He wished to use these natives as an example. On February 25, 1643, Kieft ordered an attack on the two groups, despite the pleas of the former council leader, David De Vries, who sat with the governor at his kitchen table.

At about midnight, piercing screams shattered the still of night. De Vries ran out to the ramparts of the fort and looked over to Pavonia. He saw flashes of gunfire and heard more screams. He returned to the house and sat uneasily by the fire, unable to sleep. Then there appeared a certain Native American and his wife at the door. He knew them well; they lived about an hour's walk north of his house in New Jersey. The two had jumped into a small boat and rowed across the river to New Amsterdam to escape a surprise attack by natives from Fort Orange. They sought shelter in the safety of the fort. De Vries told them that it wasn't natives who had attacked but the

Willem Kieft.

Dutch. The fort, rather than being a safe haven, would be the worst possible place to stay. He begged them to hurry and leave the area before it was too late; he led them out of the fort and they ran off into the woods.

De Vries later wrote that many Native Americans were "massacred in a manner to move a heart of stone." All told, more than 100 natives were massacred while they slept. Though Kieft had asked that women and children be spared, all were killed with severe cruelty. Those who had escaped into the bushes that night emerged the next morning only to be killed.

The colonists were unhappy that Kieft had defied them. War with the Native Americans would cripple their fur trade and endanger their lives. Colonists all across New Netherland were killed and their homes, crops, and livestock destroyed. Safety could only be assured within and around the walls of Fort Amsterdam; the isolated farms to the north were targets for nighttime strikes by natives.

Anne Hutchinson, a refugee from Massachusetts, and six of her children were killed by natives in the Bronx on isolated land Kieft had given her. Several members of the 35-family Throgmorton settlement in the Bronx were also killed. The settlement at Maspeth (Queens) was wiped out during Kieft's War, and the village's founder, Reverend Francis Doughty, fled to New Amsterdam. Gravesend (Brooklyn) was attacked but survived.

The fighting continued into 1644. Kieft's War was becoming expensive and very destructive; it nearly bankrupt the colony. Kieft proposed taxes on beaver skins and beer, to the outrage of the citizens.

The tide turned in 1644 when Captain John Underhill, a hired Englishman, arrived with reinforcements. Combining his forces with newly arrived Dutch soldiers, he raided a Native American settlement in Connecticut at night, killing hundreds. Hundreds more were killed soon after in another raid north of Manhattan. By the summer of 1645, both sides were ready for peace. A treaty was negotiated in August 1645. Kieft and the representatives of several native tribes held a ceremony in front of Fort Amsterdam.

Most of the farms in Manhattan had been damaged or destroyed during the war. The colonists were angry, and a petition of complaint against Kieft was smuggled to Holland in the fall of 1644. It ultimately got him fired.

Kieft died in 1647 when the ship carrying him back to Holland was wrecked near England.

Occasional attacks continued for years afterward. The council wrote in 1656 that "sad experiences have ... shown, that the separate dwellings of the country people, built plainly against the orders and good intentions of the Company ... have led to the murders of people, the killing of cattle and burning of houses by the savage natives of this country." It ordered isolated settlers to form hamlets and villages or be fined.

New Amsterdam circa 1651, as shown in a 1671 drawing.

NOVUM AMSTERODAMUM

Peter Stuyvesant

OF ALL the Dutch governors, Kieft's replacement, Peter Stuyvesant (1612–1672), is perhaps the best remembered. Stuyvesant arrived in May 1647 from the West Indies, where he had been governor. Having lost his leg during an attack on the Portuguese island of St. Martin, he walked with the assistance of a wooden leg. Adrien Van der Donck said that his arrival was "peacock like, with great state and pomposity."

Peter Stuyvesant.

In his first address to the people, he said he would rule "like a father over his children."

Stuyvesant developed a reputation for being stern. If anyone opposed his views, he burst forth into a dreadful rage. In 1650, Stuyvesant was ordered to appear in Amsterdam to report on the condition of his city, but he refused, saying "I shall do as I please." When, in 1653, an assembly composed of two deputies from each village in New Netherland demanded reforms, Stuyvesant ordered them to disperse, saying, "We derive our authority from God and the company, not from a few ignorant subjects."

Stuyvesant issued a proclamation in the 1650s calling for the punishment of anyone housing Quakers, and in response, settlers in Vlissingen (Flushing, Queens) composed a complaint that became known as the Flushing Remonstrance, in which they wrote, "We are bounde by the law of God and man to doe good unto all men and evil to noe man."

Stuyvesant often complained about the "decayed fortress, formerly in fair condition" being "trodden down by hogs, goats and sheep" climbing along its walls.

By 1653, when England and Holland were at war, Stuyvesant feared an attack from New England. He ordered the building of an east/west wall across Manhattan Island, at present-day Wall Street. Twelve-foot-high sharpened palisades were driven three feet into

Create a Dutch Fireplace Tile

THE TYPICAL Dutch cottage was built of wood with red roof tiles for the steeply pitched step-gabled roofs. (A 1657 city law banned thatched roofs as a fire hazard.) The more expensive homes used glazed black or yellow bricks for the end facing the street. Many of the houses featured their date of construction in iron numbers above the entry. Roofs bore attractive weather vanes. The front door was split in half horizontally, and the top featured a large brass knocker. Around these houses were cornfields and cabbage gardens. Many residents owned chickens, cows, pigs, and horses. There were plentiful orchards growing apples, peaches, pears, and mulberries. One 17th-century visitor said he had never seen, even in the best growing seasons in Europe, "such overflowing abundance."

Homes typically consisted of two rooms: a kitchen and a parlor. The kitchen also served as the living room. The parlor, its floor coated with white sand, was used mainly to entertain guests and was otherwise kept shut. The homes of the wealthy New Amsterdam residents featured fireplaces tiled with decorative blue-on-white ceramic designs. These tiles, imported from Holland (along with the yellow bricks for the exterior), were commonly used in the homeland. Designs featured everything from flowers to animals, people, mythical creatures, and ships.

What You Need

+ Scrap paper and pencil
+ 4 light-colored tiles, at least 3 inches square (from a craft store or a kitchen/bathroom store; if you can't find tiles, use 5-inch squares of foam core)
+ Fine artist's paintbrush
+ Medium to dark blue oil paint

Before you start, study the example on this page. Most Dutch tiles featured a main image in the center, with or without a decorative border. In the four corners were small flowers or decorative elements. Sometimes the tiles were designed such that patterns were revealed when many were placed together.

Draw four tiles in a square on the scrap paper and sketch some ideas. When you're ready, carefully transfer your design to the tiles with the paintbrush.

A 17th-century Dutch tile.

A 1936 poster about the Rattle Watch.

the ground, with posts to which rails were attached. A sloping reinforcement was laid against the inner wall of the palisade. At one point, several citizens were reprimanded for taking parts of the wall to use as firewood.

The brief "Peach War" came in September 1655, when over 1,500 Native Americans landed 64 canoes on Manhattan and rioted, seeking to avenge the murder of a native woman killed for stealing peaches from a Dutchman's orchard. Luckily, only a few Dutch settlers were killed.

Between 1656 and 1660, Stuyvesant had most of the city's 17 streets paved with cobblestones, the first one being Stone Street. In 1658, the city's first police brigade was created, called the "Rattle Watch." It consisted of eight men equipped with loud rattles, who were on duty from 9 PM until dawn, looking for any suspicious activities or fires. In 1674, the force was increased to 16 members, and a year later to 28. What was left of the wall came down in 1699. By then the Native Americans were no longer a threat.

The Outer Boroughs

BOTH DUTCH and English colonists settled in other parts of what is now New York City during the 17th century.

Brooklyn, across the East River from Manhattan, was very Dutch. Although Gravesend was founded by the Lady Deborah Moody, who was from England, Breuckelen (Brooklyn), New Amersfoort, Bushwick, Midwout, and New Utrecht were all Dutch settlements.

In northern Queens, there was Flushing, established in 1654 by a group of English settlers. In west-central Queens was Middleburgh (later Newtown), established in 1642 by Englishmen. In eastern Queens was Rustdorp (later Jamaica), a settlement on a plain that was ideal for grazing animals.

Both the Bronx and Staten Island were also settled, but quite sparsely, during the Dutch rule of the colony.

Stuyvesant Surrenders

THE ENGLISH wanted New Netherland from the start. In 1627, Governor Bradford of the Plymouth Colony claimed in a letter to Governor Minuit that the English owned Manhattan. As time passed and the colony grew, the English became more restless to claim this territory. In 1663, the Connecticut legislature said it would not recognize New Netherland as a legitimate Dutch colony. King Charles II granted the territory of New Netherland to his brother, the duke of York, whose mission it then was to go and claim the land for England.

In the summer of 1664, a fleet of four ships armed with 450 men and 92 guns set sail from London. On August 30, the newly arrived English forces dispatched a letter to the governor demanding surrender, promising life and liberty to all who would submit to the king's authority. Stuyvesant proclaimed that he would rather be carried off dead than surrender. He read the letter before the council but then tore it to pieces. The nervous citizens who had assembled around City Hall shouted, "The letter! The letter!" and, returning to the council chamber, he gathered up the fragments and gave them to the citizens.

Stuyvesant sent a defiant answer to the British and ordered the troops to prepare for an attack, but after 93 citizens petitioned him to surrender, he angrily gave in and signed the surrender on September 8, 1664. No shots were fired. Richard Nicolls (1624–1672) became the first British governor of the colony.

Stuyvesant went back to Holland but returned to New York four years later and died on his farm in 1672. He is buried under St. Mark's Church-in-the-Bowery (131 East 10th Street), which was originally the site of a family chapel Stuyvesant had built on his property.

Stuyvesant's Pear Tree and the Hangman's Elm

When he arrived in New Amsterdam in 1647, Governor Stuyvesant planted a pear tree on his farm at what is today Third Avenue and 13th Street. The tree bore fruit for over 200 years and finally met its end after a carriage accident in 1867.

The oldest living tree in Manhattan is an English elm located in the northwest corner of Washington Square Park. The so-called Hangman's Elm dates to 1679 and is rumored to be a tree from which people were hung in centuries past.

Stuyvesant's pear tree as it appeared in the 19th century.

The Hangman's Elm still stands in Washington Square Park.

Dutch Again

SOON AFTER the British takeover of New Amsterdam, a naval war broke out between the English and the Dutch. In May 1672, Governor Francis Lovelace called on the inhabitants for assistance in bringing the fort into a condition of defense. The English residents were eager to help, but the Dutch were not so interested in protecting themselves against invasion by their mother country.

In March 1673, news came that a Dutch fleet was sailing across the Atlantic, bound first for Virginia and then for New York. Once again, the fort was shored up and troops were brought from all around the province. But no enemy appeared, so the governor disbanded the troops and departed on a visit to other British colonies, leaving Captain John Manning in charge of the fort.

The Dutch fleet of 21 ships entered the harbor on July 28, 1673, and on July 30 summoned the fort and landed about 800 men on the Hudson River shore above the outskirts of the city. Hearing of the enemy's landing, Captain Manning sent a flag of truce and surrendered, again without a single shot being fired, and the Dutch took possession. The name of the city was changed to New Orange and the fort was renamed to Fort William Hendrick. On September 19, 1673, Anthony Colve was appointed governor.

The second Dutch administration was short-lived. When peace was proclaimed between the English and the Dutch on March 6, 1674, New Netherland was conceded to the English. On July 9, Governor Colve officially announced at the Stadt Huys (City Hall) that he had to surrender the province. Articles of capitulation were signed on September 7, and on November 19, Colve formally gave New Netherland over to the new English governor, Edmund Andros (1637–1714). The city was once again New York, and the fort was Fort James.

Stuyvesant surrenders.

Archaeology in Your Backyard

HISTORIC ARTIFACTS have been turning up in New York for hundreds of years. During the demolition of Fort George in 1789, Dutch pipes, an old brass-hilted sword, and a coin dating to 1605 were found. Over the years, hundreds of thousands of artifacts have been discovered around the city. The African Burial Ground near City Hall was discovered in 1991 during excavations for a new office building. In 2010 and 2011, large pieces of an 18th-century British ship were discovered near the World Trade Center site. City archaeologists often have to work quickly to rescue artifacts so that building construction remains on schedule.

In this activity, you will try your hand at an excavation.

What You Need
+ Tape measure
+ 4 long nails (3 inches or more) or 12-inch wooden dowels
+ Hammer or mallet
+ String
+ Trowels
+ Bucket
+ Paintbrushes, various sizes
+ Notebook
+ Camera
+ Small sandwich bags

+ Permanent marker
+ Flat-bottomed sieve

Find a spot in your backyard or schoolyard (with the school's permission) where you can dig. Measure out a 2-foot-by-2-foot square. Mark the corners with nails or dowels hammered almost all the way into the ground, and tie string from one corner to the next.

Scrape away at the surface of the ground using a trowel. Remove the loose dirt and place it into a

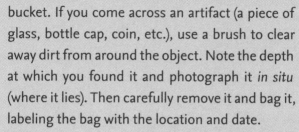

bucket. If you come across an artifact (a piece of glass, bottle cap, coin, etc.), use a brush to clear away dirt from around the object. Note the depth at which you found it and photograph it *in situ* (where it lies). Then carefully remove it and bag it, labeling the bag with the location and date.

As you continue to scrape away, you will notice the soil changing color. This is called *stratigraphy*, or layering of the soil. Note the depth at which the change occurs and the color of each layer in your notebook. When you reach a new layer, empty the bucket into the sifter and sift to find any small artifact fragments.

Keep digging until you have gone down about one foot. By now you are probably at a level representing the surface hundreds of years ago. When you are done, refill the hole.

The foundations of the Lovelace Tavern (1670) were discovered in 1979 during construction of the Goldman Sachs Building.

3

An English Colony

NEW YORK IN the 1670s was a small settlement with only about 400 houses. The English wanted New York to thrive just like Philadelphia and Boston, so Governor Andros enacted the Bolting Act in 1678 to encourage trade in the city. The law gave the city a monopoly over the flour-making business, prohibiting the making and *bolting* (sifting) of flour in any place in New York colony except the city, "nor noe flower or bread to be imported into this city, from any other part of the Province, under penalty of forfeiture." The law had major effects. Flour mills sprang up all over the city.

After communities outside the city protested and the Bolting Act was repealed in 1694, the city's merchants objected, claiming that if the repeal were allowed to stand, "many families in New York must perish" because the repeal would destroy "no less than the livelihood of all the inhabitants." But in reality, there was a flour shortage, and the city was too large by this time to support itself solely with city-milled flour. Anyway, the law had served its purpose. When it was first enacted, there were only 18 ships docked on the piers; by 1694, there were 162 ships. Flour processed in New York was shipped to places such as the West Indies, where it was traded for rum and molasses. The number of houses in New York increased from 343 in 1678 to 594 in 1696.

In 1685, a visitor named William Byrd wrote:

Its a prety pleasant towne consisting of about 700 Houses, and a very handsome strong forte wherein is the Governors House, a great Church, Secretary's office, and convenient Lodgings for the officers and Soldiers of the Garrison. . . . The Inhabitants are about six eighths Dutch, the remainder French and English. They have as many Sects of religion there as att Amsterdam, all being tolerated, yet the people seem not concerned what religion their Neighbour is of, or whether hee hath any or none.

The Dongan Charter and the Leisler Rebellion

COLONEL THOMAS Dongan (1634–1715) arrived in 1683, replacing Governor Andros, and immediately set to work drafting an official municipal charter for the city. Called the Dongan Charter, this document was approved by New York's first legislative assembly, which took place at Fort James in October 1683 and was attended by 17 representatives. The Dongan Charter was so well done it served as the foundation for New York City government for hundreds of years.

Under Dongan's rule, the official seal of New York was adopted. Modified from an ear-

Governor Edmund Andros.

New York City in the late 17th century.

Beaver Street, late 17th century.

lier version, the new seal featured two beavers, a windmill, and two barrels of flour.

Colonel Dongan, like King James II, was Catholic in a city of mainly Protestants. People were suspicious that Dongan was going to try to spread Catholicism in New York. He tried to ease fears by appointing mainly Protestants to his council and displaying religious tolerance, but he was recalled by England in August 1688 and resigned his command to Francis Nicholson, the deputy of Sir Edmund Andros (governor of both New England and New York).

Soon after, the mail from England brought startling news: King James had been overthrown by his daughter Mary and her husband William, Prince and Princess of Orange, both Protestants. English colonists realized that appointments made by the former king were now null and void. In Boston, the citizens rose up and seized Andros and had him deported back to England. In New York, however, there was uncertainty. Some folks wanted to await instruction from England (especially the council members, who had been appointed by the authority of King James), while others wanted to take immediate action. The people did not trust Nicholson, who was also Catholic. There was a rumor that the Catholics planned to attack

The official seal of New York City looked like this until 1977, when the date was changed to 1625.

the Protestants while they attended church in the fort and take over the government. The citizens wanted the militia to take control of the fort, which was where the city's treasury of £773 was stored.

In June 1689, a band of New Yorkers marched to the house of a German-born merchant named Jacob Leisler (1640–1691), senior captain of the militia, and asked him to lead them to the fort. Though he hesitated at first, Leisler eventually took a band of 47 men to the fort. There he was acknowledged as the new leader and given full power to preserve the peace and suppress any rebellion until instruction was received from England. He appointed a provisional government called the Committee of Safety. Nicholson tried to rally support but met with resistance and fled to England, leaving New York in Leisler's control.

In September, the people assembled and for the first time elected a mayor. However, the old mayor, Stephanus Van Cortlandt, still refused to step down. The new mayor held control of City Hall, while the old mayor held the charter, books, seals, and papers of New York City. Both mayors had their own common councils. It was a confusing time. In December, a commission arrived from England that authorized the person in charge as lieutenant governor, with the authority to appoint a council, until further notice. Leisler

seized the commission and proclaimed himself a legitimate ruler.

The stalemate continued for over a year. In late 1690, newly appointed governor Henry Sloughter and his retinue finally set sail from England in several ships. The first ship to arrive, in January 1691, carried Major Richard Ingoldsby, the appointed lieutenant governor. Ingoldsby demanded the immediate surrender of the fort, but Leisler refused until a royal commission was produced. This wasn't possible, since the papers were in the possession of Sloughter, who had not yet arrived.

Ingoldsby tried to rally support among the citizens, but Leisler issued a proclamation warning Ingoldsby against any hostile actions. Ingoldsby landed his troops and formed a blockade of the city both by land and sea. Leisler and his troops retreated to the fort. No hostilities followed, despite attempts to provoke Leisler. On March 19, Sloughter's ship entered the harbor. Even once Leisler was convinced that Sloughter really had arrived, he hesitated to turn himself over.

On March 30, 1691, Leisler and 11 others were tried, and on April 13, Leisler and his deputy Milborne were condemned to death as traitors. The new governor hesitated to carry out the sentence. After all, Leisler had believed he was acting on behalf of the king and queen, but Leisler's enemies were thirsty for revenge.

One day, they invited the governor to a feast and plied him with wine until they procured his signature on the death warrant.

On May 16, the sentence was carried out. Leisler's last words were, "What I have done has been but in service of my king and queen, for the Protestant cause, and for the good of my country; and for this I must die. Some errors I have committed; for these I ask pardon. I forgive my enemies as I hope to be forgiven." Four years later, England reversed the conviction and cleared his name.

Good Kidd, Bad Kidd

IN THE 17th century, piracy flourished on the high seas, and much of the booty wound up being sold in New York. Pirate captains, sometimes called privateers, visited the city quite often in those days, peddling their wares and seeking entertainment. They were easy to spot due to their colorful and exotic clothes and their gem-encrusted swords and pistols.

Piracy was such a big problem that the British government decided it was time to do something about it. It turned to Captain William Kidd (1645–1701) and made an agreement to send him out to sea as a privateer. Captain Kidd, remembered today as the most famous pirate in American history, was actually a re-

spectable resident of New York at one time. The wealthy ship's captain lived with his wife and young child in a mansion on Tienhoven Street (today Liberty Street). Among his

---

New York Place Name Origins

BUSHWICK, BROOKLYN: From Dutch *Boswijck*, meaning "little town in the woods."

FLUSHING, QUEENS: Named after Vlissingen, a settlement in southwestern Netherlands.

ASTORIA, QUEENS: Named after John Jacob Astor, who was the richest person in America at the time.

THROGS NECK, BRONX: Named after Rev. John Throckmorton or Throgmorton, an English Quaker who settled in the area in the 1640s.

TRIBECA: Triangle below Canal Street.

GREENWICH VILLAGE: Named after Greenwich, England.

CHELSEA: Named after the estate of a retired British major located between 21st and 24th Streets, from Eighth Avenue to the Hudson River.

HELL'S KITCHEN: Named by a *New York Times* reporter who in 1881 referred to a building at 551 West 39th Street as "Hell's Kitchen."

MASPETH, QUEENS: Named after the Mespeatches Indians, meaning "at the bad watering place."

HARLEM: Named after the Dutch city Haarlem.

TODT HILL, STATEN ISLAND: From the Dutch word for "dead"; a cemetery has been located there since colonial days.

FLATBUSH, BROOKLYN: From *'t Vlacke bos*, meaning "wooded plain" in Dutch.

JAMAICA, QUEENS: From Jameco, the name of the Native American tribe that lived there.

possessions were four feather beds, four tables, four dozen chairs, a Turkish carpet, and three chests of drawers.

Kidd was given an armed ship and authorized to round up a crew. After he left New York for Madagascar in 1696, Kidd made no captures for over a year. Then word began to filter back to New York that the supposed pirate chaser had given into temptation and turned pirate himself. In 1698, he captured an Armenian vessel called the *Quidagh Merchant*, yielding £64,000 of treasure. In 1699, Kidd buried part of his treasure on Gardiner's Island (off the coast of Long Island) and went to Boston but was caught and questioned. He was then arrested and sent to London, where he was found guilty of several serious charges and hanged in 1701.

Slave Rebellion of 1712 and the Panic of 1741

BY THE early 18th century, slaves were being imported into New York from both the West Indies and coastal Africa. Under British rule, the slave population continued to rise. In 1712, about two dozen slaves decided to obtain their freedom by rebelling against the whites in New York and killing as many as they could. They assembled in the orchard of a cooper named John Crooke and set fire to his outhouse. They then used guns, knives, and clubs to kill nine men who came to try to put out the fire. They fled to the woods once soldiers from the fort arrived, but about 20 were caught and executed.

The rebellion did not stop the flow of slaves into New York. By 1741, 2,000 out of the city's 11,000 inhabitants were slaves. On February 28, 1741, a Broad Street merchant named Robert Hogg was robbed of silverware, coins, and

A fanciful image of Captain Kidd in New York.

linens. One of the merchant's customers, a slave—the actual thief—told authorities that some other slaves who frequented a local tavern were responsible. Some of the stolen goods were found in a pigpen behind the Hughson Tavern. A 16-year-old white servant of the tavern, Mary Burton, blamed the owner, John Hughson, and another servant girl in the place, as well as a few slaves.

On the afternoon of March 18, the roof of the governor's home in the fort—which by now had been renamed Fort George—caught fire. That day, a plumber had been working to solder the roof's gutter, and the blaze was probably due to windblown sparks from the plumber's coal-filled firepot. Had quick-thinking men not tossed the colony's records out the window, they would surely have been burned. A strong wind caused the flames to quickly spread to the old church next door, then to nearby barracks, and finally outside the fort to some stables.

A week later, another roof in the city caught fire (probably a chimney mishap), and the week after that a storehouse with wooden boards and hay went up in flames, this time likely due to the embers from a pipe that set the hay afire. On April 4, two more fires were reported. The fires continued, more roofs caught fire, and so did the public's imagination. The citizens began to suspect a slave conspiracy.

Landfill Game

LOWER **M**ANHATTAN was much smaller when the Dutch founded New Amsterdam. Over the course of the years, landfill was added both east and west to increase the size by 25 percent.

What You Need
+ Photocopier
+ Scissors
+ 12-inch-by-20-inch aluminum pan
+ 5 pounds of modeling clay
+ Large pitcher of water
+ Broken-up peanut shells
+ Chopped-up pieces of Styrofoam
+ Some pebbles
+ 1 medium-sized bag of potting soil
+ Toy car

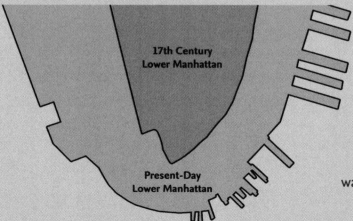

17th Century
Lower Manhattan

Present-Day
Lower Manhattan

Make a photocopy of the map on this page, enlarged to about 10 inches wide. Cut out the outline of present-day lower Manhattan and lay it on the bottom of the pan, in the center.

Using clay 2 inches deep, create Manhattan of the 17th century according the outline on the map. Now fill the pan with water so the water level is about ½ inch below the clay surface. Lay down a mixture of peanut shells, Styrofoam bits, and pebbles in the water to match the current outline of lower Manhattan. Add potting soil to the top until you have a surface that is level with the original clay.

You've just added Battery Park City on the west and Water Street, Front Street, and South Street on the east. Judging from your experiment, do you think it was easy to get the new landfill areas of Manhattan to be stable and usable? Imagine how hard this process was before there were dump trucks, when wheelbarrows were all that was available.

The panic was so great that on April 11, the city council offered a reward of £100 to anyone who had information about a plot to burn down New York. In May, Mary Burton gave testimony that meetings had been held at the Hughson Tavern, where the owner and his wife, another servant girl, a schoolteacher, and several slaves had plotted to burn down the city and take over the government. Her "confession" caused quite a stir and resulted in a serious manhunt for suspicious slaves and any whites who might be a part of the plot.

Rumors flew and gossip spread throughout the city as more and more arrests were made.

A total of 20 white people and 154 slaves were arrested; of these, 18 slaves were burned at the stake, at the present junction of Pearl and Chatham Streets; 20 were hung on an island in the Collect Pond; 78 were transported out of the city; and 50 were set free.

The Collect Pond and Lispenard's Meadows

ONE OF the most famous landmarks in New Amsterdam and colonial New York City was the Collect Pond—Kolch Pond in Dutch. Lo-

The Collect Pond in the 18th century, as drawn in 1858.

cated at present-day Franklin, Leonard, and Anthony Streets and Centre Street, the pond covered over 50 acres and was about 40 or 50 feet deep at its deepest. It was fed by several springs and had outlets on both the east and west sides leading to the East River and the Hudson River. It was a scenic place and a popular spot for skating and fishing in the Dutch era. Along with the adjacent "tea springs," it was a source of fresh water for early residents. By the mid-18th century, tanners, brewers, distilleries, and slaughterhouses were moving in along the shores of the pond and discharging their waste by-products into it.

Northwest of the Collect Pond was Lispenard's Meadows, originally a 70-acre saltwater swamp that was a place where cattle were sometimes lost because they got caught in the muck. It was covered with bushes and small trees, contained stagnant water, and smelled rotten. Between 1727 and 1739, several people who lived near the swamp suffered from fevers and other illnesses, and their doctor claimed it was due to the "unwholesome damps and vapours arising from said swamp."

 ACTIVITY

Zenger Mock Trial

THE CITY'S first newspaper, the pro-England *New York Gazette*, was founded in 1725 by William Bradford, at 60 Beaver Street. John Peter Zenger (1697–1746), a German immigrant, founded the second newspaper, the *New-York Weekly Journal*, in 1733. This newspaper was critical of English rule and its laws, which seemed unfair to the colonists.

Governor William Cosby (1690–1736), irritated at the newspaper's articles, ordered the *Journal* shut down. In a proclamation issued in November 1734, Governor Cosby said the *Journal* contained "Scandalous, Virulent, False, and Seditious Reflections" about the government. He offered a £50 reward to whoever discovered the author of those articles and had Zenger arrested.

At the trial in 1735, Zenger was defended by the illustrious Philadelphia lawyer Andrew Hamilton. In his argument before the jury, Hamilton said:

Men who injure and oppress the people under their administration provoke them to cry out and complain, and then make that very complaint the foundation for new oppressions and prosecutions... the question before the Court and you, gentlemen of the jury... is not the cause of a poor printer, nor of New York alone which you are now trying. No! It may, in its consequences, affect every freeman that lives under the British government upon the main of America. It is the best cause; it is the cause of liberty.

When he finished his argument, the spectators applauded. The jury deliberated for just a few minutes and returned a verdict of not guilty to a round of cheers. The next day, the city gave a dinner in Hamilton's honor.

In this activity, you will reenact part of the Zenger trial. Assign parts to lawyers for both sides, Zenger, the judge, and the jury. You can go to www.courts.state.ny.us/history/zenger.htm for the original transcript, then select the parts you want to reenact or read it over and create your own kid-friendly version.

Burning of Zenger's newspapers, 1734.

Revolutionary New York

N EW YORK CITY in the mid-18th century was a bustling seaport. By 1760, there were 2,600 houses in the city, and it had a population of 18,000. It was now of comparable size and importance to Philadelphia and Boston.

One important development in the city was the chartering of King's College in 1754, on land owned by Trinity Church. Classes were first held in a building adjacent to the church. The fifth of nine colleges chartered by the British in the colonies, King's College (later renamed Columbia University) had an initial enrollment of eight students.

❮ **The toppling of the King George statue, 1776.**

St. Paul's Chapel was built in 1766 on Wall Street. George Washington worshipped there

One of its most famous students entered in 1774: future secretary of the treasury and vice president Alexander Hamilton.

Commerce thrived. By 1771, the sloops of the Hudson River had become large, powerful boats, and there were 125 sailing between Albany and New York. Merchant ships departing New York in the 1760s and '70s carried flour, apples, poultry, onions, and lumber, among other things, to the West Indies and returned with rum and sugar. As the shipping business grew, many new warehouses were built along the waterfront to store soon-to-be shipped or recently arrived commodities.

The Stamp Act

NEW YORKERS in the mid-1760s were unhappy with new colonial laws, especially the Stamp Act, which required that taxes be paid on everything from newspapers to playing cards. Special tax stamps had to be purchased and affixed to the goods. For the many merchants in the city (and throughout the colonies), this was unacceptable and unfair.

News spread that the act was set to take effect on November 1, 1765, and on October 7, a special congress was convened in New York, consisting of 28 representatives from nine colonies. When asked for his support, the acting governor, Lieutenant Governor Cadwallader Colden (1688–1776), refused. He called the congress "unconstitutional, unprecedented, and unlawful."

When the stamps arrived in New York on October 23, there was nobody to deliver them to, since the appointed stamp collector had resigned a few days earlier. Colden ordered that the stamps be brought to him in the fort. After a little over two weeks, the Stamp Act Congress issued a Declaration of Rights that formally listed their complaints and beliefs. It was a precursor to the Declaration of Independence.

On October 31, about 200 city merchants met at Burns' Coffee House and signed a resolution condemning the act. They agreed not to order anything from England until the Stamp Act was repealed.

Despite the armed ships in the harbor, the people revolted. A mob of angry New Yorkers, many of whom were members of the Sons of Liberty, a patriotic society organized by Isaac Sears, marched to the fort carrying an *effigy* (a crude dummy) of Colden holding a stamped paper. When they reached the lieutenant governor's stable just outside the fort, they dragged out his coach and placed the effigy inside. The rioters then pushed the coach to Bowling Green, where they ripped down the wooden fence around the green, threw it around the coach, and set the whole thing ablaze.

On November 5, an armed band of citizens gathered at the Commons (City Hall Park) and resolved to storm the fort and take hold of the stamp papers by force. The governor finally yielded and appeared at the fort gate to give the stamps to the mayor, John Cruger. The seven packages of stamp papers and parchments came with a letter from Colden that said he was giving up the stamps "to prevent the . . . blood and the calamities of a civil war which might ensue from my withholding them from you."

In mid-November, a second shipment of stamps arrived from England, along with a new stamp distributor and governor. The new governor, Sir Henry Moore, wanted nothing to do with the stamps, which were delivered to City Hall to join the original seven packages. The new stamp distributor quickly resigned once he realized that the atmosphere was hostile. The Sons of Liberty heard that more stamps were on board a ship that was stopped in New York but bound for Connecticut. They boarded the ship and found and seized 10 packages of stamps, took them to the shipyards at the foot of Catherine Street, and burned them.

The British government, wary of the colonists' revolts, repealed the Stamp Act on February 20, 1766. When the news reached New York on May 20, the people rejoiced. Bells were rung, cannons were fired, and the citizens lit a bonfire at Bowling Green. For the occasion, the Sons of Liberty erected a tall wooden "Liberty Pole" in the Common carrying a large banner that said "George III. Pitt & Liberty." William Pitt was a member of the British Parliament who had defended the colonies and declared that Britain had no right to tax them.

On June 4, King George III's birthday, some of the colonists were again in a mood to celebrate. They assembled, and the governor saw to it that an ox was roasted, 25 barrels of beer were provided, and 25 cannons were fired in salute. A group of pleased citizens gathered at Burns' Coffee House and petitioned the

Above: Defending the Liberty Pole, 1767.

Right: Burning of the tax stamps in New York, 1765.

Erect a Liberty Pole

IN MARCH 1767, when the Sons of Liberty found that their third Liberty Pole had been cut down, they erected a fourth one. One night, three years later, the soldiers pulled down the fourth pole and sawed it into pieces. They piled the pieces in front of the door of the house where the Sons of Liberty held their meetings.

People were enraged the next morning, January 18, 1770. A crowd gathered in the fields and fighting broke out between members of the crowd and some British soldiers. The soldiers fell back to Golden Hill, at the corner of John and William Streets. They then charged with their bayonets on the crowd, whose only weapons were stones, clubs, and knives. One citizen was killed and several were wounded at the Battle of Golden Hill, the first bloodshed of the American Revolution.

In this activity, you'll make and erect your own Liberty Pole.

What You Need
+ Sketching paper and pencil
+ Piece of light-colored fabric (solid color), 3 feet by 2 feet minimum
+ Scissors
+ Fabric markers, in multiple colors
+ Embroidery thread, in multiple colors (optional)
+ Needle (optional)
+ Grommet kit (optional)
+ String
+ Wooden broom or pole
+ Glue

Develop a design for your banner. It can be the word "Liberty" or "Say No to the Stamp Act" or something else along those lines. The key is to remember that you will be sending a message to your fellow patriots who pass by the Common.

Cut the fabric into a banner shape—an elongated triangle. Carefully transfer your design to the banner and use fabric pens to write letters, decorate it, and color it. If you are feeling more adventurous, you can try embroidering your message on the fabric using colored embroidery thread.

If you have a grommet kit, you can attach two grommets to the fabric, insert string, and then tie it tightly around the top of the pole. If not, use scissors to carefully make holes about 3 inches from the base of the banner. You may need a little glue to secure the string to the pole.

assembly to erect an equestrian statue of the king. On August 10, British soldiers cut down the Liberty Pole, but two days later the Sons of Liberty erected another. There were a total of five Liberty Poles erected between 1766 and 1776. In 1921, a 66-foot-high ceremonial Liberty Pole was erected on the site.

It took three years for the statue of the king to arrive from London. It was erected at Bowling Green on August 21, 1770, and enclosed by an iron fence. Toasts were made to His Majesty's health and cannons were fired at the Battery, accompanied by a band. The good feelings did not last too long, as anti-British sentiment grew. In 1773, it was decreed that anyone caught defacing the statue would have to pay a fine of £500 or be thrown in prison for a year.

Rising Tensions

UPON HEARING the news of the battles of Lexington and Concord in April 1775, New York's patriots banded together and stormed City Hall and the Custom House, taking control of city government and distributing arms to the citizens. There were still plenty of loyalists (those who still supported the British) in town, but for the moment the patriots had control. And they made the most of it.

In January 1776, Colonel Nathaniel Heard took 900 soldiers to Queens to disarm suspected Tories (loyalists). Colonel Heard imposed an oath of loyalty on 471 people, disarmed 349 others, and carried away almost 1,000 muskets.

Others continued this effort. Lieutenant Colonel Isaac Sears wrote in March 1776, "Yesterday I arrived at Newtown . . . and tendered the oath to four of the greatest Tories, which they swallowed as hard as if it was a four pound shot they were trying to get down. . . . The houses are so scattered it is impossible to catch many without horses to ride after them; but I shall exert myself to catch the greatest part of the ringleaders."

In May 1776, some school boys in Newtown hoisted a large flag "in imitation of the King's standard" on a high pole in the yard of John Moore, the man with whom they were boarding. For allowing this insult to the patriots to occur, Moore was arrested and detained in New York.

In July 1776, Reverend Joshua Bloomer of Jamaica was ordered to omit prayers for the king during services in his church. Rather than do this, he closed his church for five Sundays in a row.

A 1775 print shows a patriotic New York barber refusing to finish shaving a British officer.

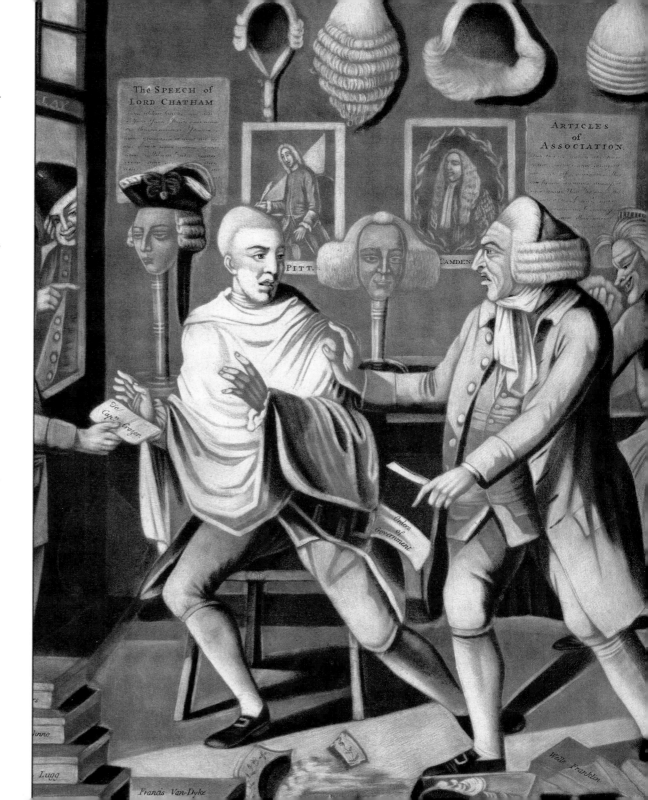

The Finest Apple in America

The most famous apple of the colonial era originated in what is now Elmhurst, Queens. The original seedling tree of the Newtown Pippin apple stood near a swamp on the estate of Gershom Moore, in what was then called Newtown, from the early years of the 18th century until it died in about 1805.

The Newtown Pippin was the first American apple to attract notice in Europe. The first Pippins shipped overseas went to none other than Benjamin Franklin. It was said to be George Washington's favorite apple. Thomas Jefferson began growing Pippins on his estate in Virginia by 1778. Known for its sweet-tart taste and its ability to be kept for up to nine months, the Pippin was called the finest apple the United States ever produced.

The yellow Newtown Pippin, first cultivated in Queens.

On July 9, 1776, after listening to a reading of the Declaration of Independence, a band of about 40 men went to Bowling Green, used ropes to topple the statue of King George from its pedestal, and dragged it through the streets. They beheaded the statue and lopped off its nose. Then, since it was made of lead, the statue was shipped to Litchfield, Connecticut, where it was melted and cast into 42,000 bullets. Connecticut soldiers supposedly used these bullets to kill 400 British soldiers during

A crownless Bowling Green fence post.

the war. The crowns topping the posts of the iron Bowling Green railings were hacked off that night by the angry mob.

The Battle of Long Island

THE PATRIOTS of New York would not enjoy victory for long. After the British evacuation of Boston in March, the British quickly built up the force necessary for a full-scale invasion of New York. Washington arrived in New York in April and immediately ordered the construction of fortifications in upper Manhattan. Another part of Washington's army was busy constructing fortifications in Brooklyn Heights.

Meanwhile the British were using Staten Island as a staging area for more than 30,000 soldiers. An attack was coming soon. On August 22, 1776, 15,000 British troops and Hessian mercenaries (German soldiers hired by the British to fight the Americans) ferried from Staten Island to Utrecht (Gravesend Bay, Brooklyn). They disembarked without opposition, along with 40 cannons, in two and a half hours. The few Americans along the coast retreated to fortified Brooklyn Heights, where their forces were concentrated (present-day Prospect Park). The British marched eastward, south of the American line, and snuck 10,000 troops through an undefined pass near Jamaica, attacking the Americans from the rear. The Americans fought back but were outnumbered and overpowered.

On the night of August 29, the Americans silently evacuated their positions and slipped across the East River to Manhattan in small boats, escaping under the cover of rain and fog. As one regiment left its position, the remaining troops fanned out to fill the vacancies, keeping the campfires burning so nothing appeared strange to the British sentries.

Washington's escape was critical; had the Americans been further engaged, the war may have ended right there. Washington decided to evacuate much of his army from the city and, leaving only about 3,000 troops there, he brought the rest to Harlem Heights.

The Americans escape from Brooklyn in August 1776.

The *Turtle*: First Submarine

IN THE spring of 1776, Washington authorized a Connecticut mechanic and inventor named David Bushnell to use an ingenious one-man submarine he had developed to attack the British. This vessel, called the *Turtle*, was made of tarred oak with a brass hatch just big enough for one man to slip through.

The oval-shaped *Turtle* had 200 pounds of lead on the bottom, called a *ballast*, which could be raised or lowered at will to allow the submarine to sink or rise to the surface. The operator had to control the rudder and operate a hand crank that turned the propeller in front. The machine was also equipped with a screw meant for drilling into a ship's hull, to which a torpedo of sorts would be fastened. This explosive was actually made out of two hollowed-out pieces of oak and filled with 150 pounds of gunpowder and a fused timer device that would set off the explosion a few minutes later, after the submarine made its escape. Small windows at the top allowed the operator to navigate.

After a few trials, the vessel was deemed ready for action and smuggled by land to New York. On the night of September 6, 1776, it was put in the water near Whitehall Street. Its target was the 64-gun British frigate the *Eagle*, anchored off Governor's Island. Piloted

Drawing of David Bushnell's *Turtle*.

by Sergeant Ezra Lee, the *Turtle* successfully reached the *Eagle* and descended under the stern of the ship, so close he could hear the voices of the officer on the deck above.

Lee tried to fasten the screw to the hull but hit metal and had to give up. Afraid of being detected, he steered the ship back toward Manhattan. He was spotted, and when he saw some British soldiers begin to row out toward him, he released his explosive into the water. The British retreated, the explosive detonated and sent a huge column of water skyward, and the *Turtle* was safely towed back to shore by waiting Americans.

The *Turtle* tried to attack another ship a couple of weeks later, but without success. Nevertheless, it would go down in history as the first submersible ever used on a combat mission.

The Battle of Manhattan

ON SEPTEMBER 15, just two weeks after Washington's precarious escape from Brooklyn, a large force of British soldiers descended upon the shores of the East River. There was a great thunderous noise as 70 cannons from several British warships fired at the coastline to cover

American boats engaged the British ships *Phoenix* and *Rose* on August 16, 1776, in the Hudson River.

the troops that were being sent to land. American soldiers watched with horror from their ditches near the waterfront as 84 troop-filled boats launched from Newtown Creek across the East River, under cover of the frigates. The soldiers waited quietly until the British were within firing range and the American officers ordered a retreat. Chaos ensued. One soldier recalled that "the demons of fear and disorder seemed to take full possession . . . that day."

As soon as he heard the cannon fire, General Washington mounted his horse and raced four miles from Harlem. As he arrived at approximately 40th Street and Park Avenue, he saw the panicked American troops retreating in all directions. He shouted out orders to them, telling them to form along the line of the Post Road (Lexington Avenue): "Take to the wall! Take to the cornfield!"

Nothing Washington said had any effect, and he was so frustrated with the troops that he threw his hat to the ground and exclaimed, "Are these the men with whom I am to defend America?" Not only was he disgusted, he was in a trance of disbelief, and one of his staff had to take hold of his horse's bridle and turn the animal's head in the other direction to get Washington to return to the safety of the north. Washington later wrote that he "used every means in my power to rally and to get them into some order," but the Americans "ran away in the greatest confusion, without firing a single shot."

Fifteen Americans were killed and 300 taken prisoner in the battle, but the rest finally made it to safety in Harlem. Not wishing the British to think they could so easily rout them, the Americans took the offensive the next day, heading south to meet the British forces (already on their way north to attack the Americans) around the location of present-day Columbia University. The Battle of Harlem Heights proved to be the first battle in which the Continental Army was able to force a British retreat. Only 20 or so Americans were killed or wounded.

Many loyalists remained in the city. The secretary to Admiral Richard Howe, commander of the British fleet, wrote, "Nothing could equal the expressions of joy shewn by the Inhabitants, upon the arrival of the King's officers among them. They even carried some of them upon their shoulders about the streets . . . a Woman pulled down the Rebel [flag] upon the fort, and a Woman hoisted up in its stead His Majesty's Flag, after trampling the other under Foot with the most contemptuous indignation."

The Great Fire of 1776

ALL OF New York was now preoccupied with the war that had arrived at its doorstep. Pa-triot or loyalist, all were wondering what the outcome would be. The British now occupied New York, and their troops could be seen parading about the streets every day. At the time, Broadway was a beautiful tree-lined avenue, with fine houses along its entire length. Ambrose Serle called it and Queen Street "the fairest and best built streets in the town."

Then tragedy struck. In the wee hours of September 21, just six days after the British arrived in New York, fire broke out in some wooden structures near the waterfront (around Whitehall). As the city's bells had been carried off by the American army, the alarm could not easily be sounded. (Those who blamed the "rebels" for the fire suspected that that was exactly the idea.) The British soldiers sprang out of their beds and tried to contain the flames with buckets of water from the river, but fanned by a strong south wind, the fire spread rapidly over the course of the night.

The fire spread north, up the eastern side of Broadway, engulfing everything in its path. Near Wall Street, the flames were halted by a brick house but leapt over to the western side of Broadway and wreaked havoc there as well. Flames lapped hungrily at the roof and tower of Trinity Church. The 140-foot-high steeple "resembled a vast pyramid of fire," and soon the famous building was in ruins.

City Hall Park Walking Tour

CITY HALL Park, on the site of a common that had been in use since the Dutch days, is one of the historically richest sites in the entire city.

Get an adult to accompany you and start your walking tour at (1) The Tweed Courthouse (52 Chambers Street). This infamous building was built on the site that first had British soldiers' barracks (1757–1790) and then a poorhouse (1796–1854) that later became Scudder's American Museum.

Walk west, to the corner of Broadway and Chambers Streets (2). You are now standing on the southern edge of the African Burial Ground, used in the 18th century and rediscovered by accident in the 1990s. (A visitor's center is located at 290 Broadway.)

Now walk south along Broadway until you get to the entrance to the park. There are three markers nearby. On the sidewalk are markers for the Bridewell (3), which was the site of the city jail from 1775 to 1838, and also a marker for British soldiers' barracks. Just a bit farther, within the fence, is a marker for the Liberty Pole.

Enter the park and walk to the spectacular fountain (4), which was built in the park in 1871 but relocated to the Bronx for 60 years before returning in 2000.

Next, look north to City Hall (5). When begun in 1803, it was on the northern edge of town. Massachusetts marble was used for the front and sides, but the back (north-facing side) was red sandstone, because it was thought that nothing important would be built north of that point. City Hall was built on the site of the first *almshouse*, or poorhouse, a place where poor people could go for shelter (1736–1797).

The old Post Office (6) (1870–1939) was located at the southern tip of City Hall Park. For a closer look at the back of City Hall and the back of the Tweed Courthouse, walk back north along Broadway to the passageway (7) between the two buildings.

Archaeological excavations in 1999 uncovered more than 250,000 artifacts from the various structures that used to exist within the Common.

The Post Office stood at the southern tip of City Hall Park.

It was only when the fire reached St. Paul's Chapel that the people were able to stop it. They climbed onto the roof of the church and poured buckets of water down until the flames were put out.

The fire raged for 10 hours before it was extinguished. British soldiers pulled down many wooden buildings in its path to prevent it from spreading further. According to a newspaper report in the *New-York Gazette* (which was sympathetic to the Tories), "several persons were discovered with large bundles of matches, dipped in resin and brimstone, and attempting to set fire to the houses." One man was caught cutting the handles off water buckets; he was hung until dead. Another was allegedly caught in the act of trying to spread the fire and was seized by the British and thrown into the fire.

These reports led some to believe that the fire was the work of patriots, who had resolved to burn New York rather than let the British have it. To this day, no one is certain who was to blame. About 1,000 houses were destroyed, roughly a third of the city. The once beautiful Broadway was now a street of rubble and ruins and would remain that way for the entire period of British occupation. Another fire ravaged the city in August 1778 along the docks of the East River waterfront, destroying 64 buildings.

Shown in an 18th-century print, the Fire of 1776 destroyed a third of New York City.

The Surrender of New York

THE VICTORY at Harlem Heights on September 16 was a small one. Washington knew it was too risky to keep a large force on Manhattan Island. In the autumn of 1776, he proceeded to evacuate most of his troops from the island, leaving a little more than 3,000 men encamped at Fort Washington in upper Manhattan (about 183rd Street).

In early November, with the sighting of three British ships sailing up the Hudson unharmed, General Washington realized that it would be impossible to hold Fort Washington. He gave directions to his most trusted lieutenant, General Greene, to have the fort evacuated as soon as convenient. Washington wrote:

If we cannot prevent vessels from passing up, and the enemy are possessed of the surrounding country, what valuable purpose can it answer to attempt to hold a post from which the expected benefit cannot be had? I am,

therefore, inclined to think that it will not be prudent to hazard the men and stores at Mount Washington: but, as you are on the spot, I leave it to you to give such orders as to evacuating Mount Washington, as you may judge best, and so far revoking the order given to Colonel Magaw, to defend it to the last.

Instead of evacuating, General Greene sent reinforcements to Fort Washington. On November 15, British General William Howe demanded that Magaw surrender the fort, but Magaw said he was determined "to defend this post to the very last extremity." The following day, the British began a multipronged attack with a force numbering well over 10,000. The Americans tried to hold their ground, but the British and their Hessian mercenaries pushed at them relentlessly.

General Washington watched with dismay through a telescope from across the river as the scene unfolded. When he saw the enemy send a flag into the fort to summon surrender, Washington dispatched a messenger with a note telling the fort's commander that if he could hold out until night, Washington would try to make arrangements to have the troops ferried across the river to safety. The brave messenger successfully delivered the message and then dodged the bayonets of lunging Hessians as he scampered back to his boat.

British troops parading during the occupation.

But it was too late. The enemy was too close to the fort and the Americans were too badly outnumbered. Shortly after the message was delivered, the fort was taken; around 2,600 American soldiers were captured as prisoners of war. Though there were 150 American casualties, the British had suffered 500 casualties and the Hessians 350. It would be seven long years before the Americans regained control of New York.

In September 1776, the 21-year-old American spy Nathan Hale, dressed as a schoolteacher, was captured by the British on Long Island and executed in New York, at either Vanderbilt Avenue and 44th Street or Third Avenue and 66th Street (plaques mark both spots). His last words were "I only regret that I have but one life to lose for my country."

Occupied New York

THE OCCUPATION was not pleasant for New Yorkers. No attempt was made to repair the damage done by the great fire. The British had no reason to do so. They suspected it was the work of the "rebels" anyway. The poor lived in tents and shacks littering the disaster zone, known as "Canvas Town."

Prices during the war rose 800 percent. All the churches in the city, except for the Episcopal, Methodist, and Lutheran (spared for the Hessian troops) had been converted into hospitals, prisons, barracks, or warehouses. The pews were ripped out and windows broken. Fences around the churches and graveyards were ripped out. The streets were dirty, and most commerce was at a virtual standstill.

In March 1777, General William Howe offered a full pardon to any rebels who gave up their arms, as well as the "full value" for the weapons they turned in; they would be "permitted" to enter into the king's service and fight for Britain. In April, General Howe issued another proclamation from his New York headquarters in which he said that the king had authorized him to promise 50 acres of land for privates and 200 acres for noncommissioned officers who enlisted in the royal army for two years.

About 2,000 prisoners of war were kept in wretched conditions during the war years, starved and cold, either in the city itself or on ships in the harbor.

Statue of Nathan Hale in City Hall Park.

The prison ship *Jersey*, off the east coast of Manhattan.

Evacuation Day

THE REVOLUTIONARY War ended in 1781, but without a treaty, the British still occupied New York. The governor, Sir Guy Carleton, finally received news on April 6, 1783, that an official peace treaty had been signed in Paris. This brought great joy to the patriots and disappointment to the loyalists.

Those who had fled before the British occupation began to return to the city, and loyalists began to make arrangements for their departure. About 600 of them had already left by the fall of 1782, bound mainly for Nova Scotia. On April 27, 1783, a fleet of 16 ships set sail from New York, carrying 471 loyalist families bound for Nova Scotia, other parts of Canada, and the Bahamas; more would follow. Altogether about 12,000 loyalists fled the city once peace was declared.

Noon on November 25, 1783, was set as the time for the evacuation of British troops from the city. As an old story goes, that morning Mr. Day, a tavern keeper on Murray Street, proudly hung the Stars and Stripes. The jailer, Captain William Cunningham, found out and went immediately to Day's Tavern, where he ordered, "Take in that flag, the city is ours till noon!" Mr. Day refused. Cunningham tried then to take down the flag himself, but Mrs. Day emerged from the tavern and whacked Cunningham mercilessly with her broom, causing clouds of powder to fly from his wig and forcing him to give up

The festivities began with the arrival of Major General Henry Knox, who marched with his troops from Harlem down to what is now the Bowery and Third Avenue, where he met the British forces. The British then began to march to the east, toward the river, where they boarded their ship. General Knox marched his troops triumphantly down Broadway to the cheers

Evacuation Day, November 25, 1783.

of the gathered crowds lining the streets and watching from windows and balconies. General Knox met up with a group of mounted citizens, recently returned from exile, each wearing in his hat a sprig of laurel. This group rode back uptown to the Bull's Head Tavern (on the Bowery, between present-day Bayard and Canal Streets), where General Washington and Governor Clinton were waiting.

A grand horseback procession, led by Washington and Clinton, with Knox and other officials following, was joined by a number of citizens on foot. At Chatham and Pearl Streets, General Knox and his officers marched down Chatham Street, while Washington and his company turned onto Pearl Street and then proceeded onto Wall Street, and from there to Broadway and down to the Battery, where the last formality would be to unfurl the American flag over Fort George.

A crowd was already gathered at the fort to witness the event. But though the British had taken everything else, they had left the British flag. Not only that, the ropes used for hoisting and lowering the flag had been cut away, and the flag itself had been nailed to the pole, which had been smeared with grease! Attempts to climb the slippery pole were unsuccessful, and cutting down the pole and erecting another would take too long. Someone finally ran off to a nearby hardware store and bought

ACTIVITY

Create a Walking Tour of Your Neighborhood

WE SOMETIMES get so used to our own neighborhoods that we hardly pay any attention to the details. How often do you pass by an old building with a hidden past? A school with a famous alumnus? A church with a secret history? A house that's much older than you think? What interesting facts await discovery about places within walking distance of where you live?

What You Need
+ Graph paper
+ Computer with Internet access
+ Notebook
+ Pen
+ Camera
+ Printer

Using graph paper, map out all or part of your neighborhood—at least a four-block-by-four-block area. Mark each building on the map with a rectangle or appropriate shape. To find out information on your neighborhood, there are many possible resources. If you live in New York, there are dozens of walking tour and architectural guides that have been published. Many locales (cities or counties) offer online property searches that yield information about each building (such as the date built or the previous owners' names). You can also check your local library or historical society. They'll often have old newspaper clippings, maps, photographs, and documents about your neighborhood's history.

Once your map is drawn, interview long-time neighborhood residents and ask them questions about what the area was like when they moved in or if they have any old photographs or stories about certain buildings. Compile the information into a Walking Tour flyer by numbering the buildings or sites on the map for which you have information, picking logical starting and ending points for the tour. Then fill in the historical facts you've discovered for each tour stop and add some digital photos (and maybe scans of old photos, if available).

Print out your finished flyer and you're ready to conduct your tour!

some cleats to nail onto the pole. Using these as steps, a young man named John Van Arsdale managed to work his way up the pole. With further assistance from a ladder, he was able to rip down the old flag and rig up the Stars and Stripes. A 13-gun salute followed. So pleased was the crowd that once Van Arsdale descended, hats were passed around in collection of a small reward, and as the story goes, even General Washington contributed.

Washington, Clinton, and some officers went to Fraunces Tavern at Pearl and Broad Streets, where a dinner was served and 13 toasts were drunk in celebration. In the evening the festivities continued. Rockets were fired and bonfires were lit at every corner.

On November 28, a group of recently returned New Yorkers threw a party for the governor and the city council at Cape's Tavern, with a surprise visit from General Washington and about 300 of his officers. On December 2, there was a great display of fireworks at Bowling Green.

On December 4, the British finally began to evacuate Long Island and Staten Island. That same day, General Washington bade a final farewell to his officers at Fraunces Tavern. The General filled a glass of wine and addressed his brave fellow soldiers: "With a heart full of love and gratitude I now take leave of you: I most devoutly wish that your latter days may be as prosperous and happy as your former ones have been glorious and honorable." He embraced each one of them as tears flowed freely, and then returned to his home in Virginia.

Capital City

THE REBUILDING process in New York was a slow one. After a great fire and seven years of commercial stagnation, it would take some time for the city to regroup.

The city's new mayor, James Duane (served 1784–1789), appointed commissioners to oversee the reconstruction of the destroyed area. In 1785, a merchant named John Thurman wrote, "Many of our new merchants and shopkeepers set up since the war have failed. We have nothing but complaints of bad times. . . . Very small are our exports. There is no ship building." A man named Samuel Breck wrote of his visit to New York in 1787, "I arrived at that city and found it a neglected place, built chiefly of wood, and in a state of prostration and decay. . . . Although the war had ceased during that period, and the enemy had departed, no attempt had been made to rebuild. . . . In short, there was silence and inactivity everywhere."

In 1787, the state legislature gave a go-ahead for the Common Council to lay out new streets and improve existing ones. Between the loyalists who had fled and the patriots who were returning, the city's population experienced much change over the course of a few years. New York had long been second in importance to either Boston or Philadelphia, but it was finally poised to outshine both: New York was to be the capital of the new republic!

Fort George had been demolished in 1789 to make way for a new home for the president across from Bowling Green, and construction was under way when president-elect Washington arrived in New York for his inauguration. On April 30, 1789, a long procession passed down the streets, with music, flags, guns, and loud applause. The inauguration took place on the balcony of the newly built Federal Hall on the corner of Wall Street and Nassau Street.

Federal Hall was designed by Major Pierre L'Enfant, who would later lay out the plan for Washington, DC. The inauguration filled the city with excitement, and a crowd of thousands swelled along Broadway. Washington wore a brown suit and white silk stockings, and had a steel-hilted sword at his side as he took the oath.

New York's time as capital was brief. On December 6, 1790, Philadelphia became the country's capital. The building that was to be the president's residence was put to other purposes; it served as the home of governors Clinton and Jay, and also as a custom house.

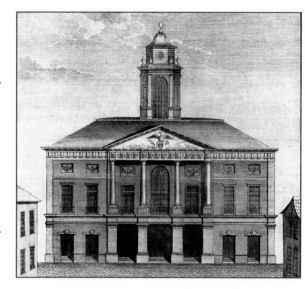

Left: Federal Hall.

Below: Washington's inauguration, 1789.

North Church   27 Fort George & Battery &c.
New Presbyterian D°   25 Fly Market
S.t George's Chapl.t   26 Oswego D°
S.t Peter's Church   27 Bear D°
The College   28 Peck's Slip D°
New Scots Meeting   29 New... D°
Old Dutch Church   30 Bridewell
New Dutch D°   31 City Alms House
Jews Synagogue   32 Prison
Old Quaker Meeting   33 Hospital
Methodist D°   34 Theatre
Baptist D°   35 Jews Burying Ground
Calvanist Church   36 Lower Barracks
                      37 Upper D°

N° 1 South Ward
   2 West D°
   3 North D°
   4 Dock D°
   5 East D°
   6 Montgomery D°
   7 Out D°

NORTH OR HUDSON RIVER

EAST RIVER

Ferry to Paules Hook

Fresh Water Pond

Boards Lane

Road to Boston

Bowery Lane

Division St.

Rutgers St.

Cherry

Catharine Slip

Oliver's Slip

Peck's Slip

Beekman Slip

Burling Slip

Old Slip

Long Is. Ferry

Battery

Broadway

Broad

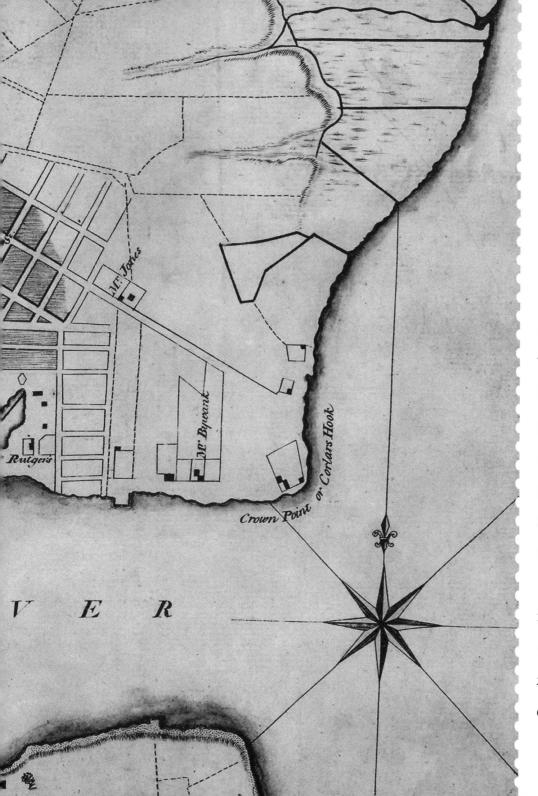

5

Merchant City

NEW YORK CITY'S population grew from 23,614 in 1786 to 30,022 in 1790, as patriots who had left made their way back and new inhabitants were attracted by the promise of a rebuilding city. Everywhere downtown there was growth and construction, yet in 1790, points as far south as Varick and Houston Streets were still "country," with great old oak trees, wild shrubs, and partridges and rabbits roaming the area. This wilderness would not last long, for the city was expanding fast, and commerce was thriving.

Commerce was the lifeblood of New York. According to legend, the New York Stock Exchange had its origins in the "Buttonwood Agreement" of 1792, when 24 brokers met under a buttonwood tree at what is now 68 Wall Street and signed a compact on the trading of stocks. Shipbuilding boomed and merchants prospered.

Between 1785 and 1805, several newspapers were founded. In 1785, the *Daily Advertiser* and *Independent Journal* were begun. In 1790, the *General Advertiser* was founded by Benjamin Franklin's grandson. In 1791, the *National Gazette* was begun, and in 1793, the *American Minerva* (later the *Globe*) was launched by Noah Webster. And in 1801, with the backing of Alexander Hamilton, the *New York Evening Post* (now the *New York Post*) was first published.

By 1801, the city's population was 60,489; by 1805 it was 75,770; and by 1807 it had climbed to 83,530. The value of exports from New York City more than quadrupled between 1803 and 1807. John Lambert, an English traveler, wrote about his visit to New York in 1807:

> *The wharfs are large and commodious, and the warehouses . . . are lofty and substantial. . . . These ranges of buildings and wharfs extend from the Grand Battery, on both sides [of] the town, up the Hudson and East rivers, and encompass the houses with shipping, whose forest of masts gives a stranger a lively idea of the immense trade which this city carries on with every part of the globe . . . the port was filled with shipping, and the wharfs were crowded with commodities of every description. Bales of cotton, wool, and merchandize; barrels*

> *of pot-ash, rice, flour, and salt provisions; hogsheads of sugar, chests of tea, puncheons of rum, and pipes of wine; boxes, cases, packs, and packages of all sizes and denominations, were strewed upon the wharfs and landing-places, or upon the decks of the shipping. All was noise and bustle. . . . Every thing was in motion. . . . The people were scampering in all directions to trade with each other, and to ship off their purchases for the European, Asian, African, and West Indian markets.*

Knickerbocker's History of New-York

WASHINGTON IRVING (1783–1859), author of "The Legend of Sleepy Hollow," published *Knickerbocker's History of New-York* in 1809. His original idea was to parody a recently published book called *A Picture of New-York*, but he decided instead to focus on the Dutch period of New York's history:

> *I was surprised to find how few of my fellow citizens were aware that New-York had ever been called New-Amsterdam. . . . This, then, broke upon me as the poetic age of our city; poetic from its very obscurity; and open, like the early and obscure days of Rome, to all embellishments of historical fiction.*

Ridley & Co. Candy Manufacturing was established in 1806 on Chambers Street, at a time when business was booming all over town.

So Irving invented a fictional narrator named Diedrich Knickerbocker and placed ads in New York newspapers seeking "a small elderly gentleman, dressed in an old black coat and cocked hat" who had disappeared from his hotel. The book came with a note from the publishers that said the manuscript was found in his hotel room and was being published to pay off some of Knickerbocker's debts.

In the book, Irving poked fun at the Dutch and invented romantic notions of the days when "New Amsterdam was a mere pastoral town, shrouded in groves of sycamores and willows, and surrounded by trackless forests and wide-spreading waters, that seemed to shut out all the cares in the world."

Many history books since 1809 have quoted Irving's book, but for the most part he was only kidding! By this time, Irving had already contributed to New York's lore by coining the name "Gotham" for the city in 1807.

Filling the Collect Pond

BY THE late 18th century, the once-scenic Collect Pond was doomed by the city's relentless northward push and the worsening quality of the pond's water. In 1766, a French engineer had proposed to make the pond into a ship basin and connect it to the Hudson and East Rivers via a canal. A complaint was registered in 1784 that people were washing their dirty linen in the pond, and in 1787 the pond was reported to be full of garbage.

In 1796, a man named John Fitch experimented with a steamboat on the pond. He fitted an 18-foot-long boat with steam-driven paddlewheels. The steam was generated in a crude boiler, consisting of an iron pot holding about 10 gallons of water. The boat, together with a portion of its machinery, was abandoned on the shore of the Collect Pond and the wood was carried away by the inhabitants of the neighborhood for fuel. In 1802, the street commissioner recommended that a canal be cut east-west to drain the pond, but nothing was done.

In 1803, work began nearby on the new City Hall. Dealing with the pond was fast becoming an urgent priority; in 1805 it was found to be filled with dead animals. Finally, in 1808, the pond was filled in, in part to give work to those who were unemployed due to a shipping embargo. The hills west of the Collect Pond were leveled and the dirt was dumped in the pond, along with garbage carted from the city. Unfortunately, because the fill was heavier than the mud at the bottom of the pond, the mud rose to the surface and formed a mound.

Today, Centre Street runs north-south through what was the middle of the pond. The

Washington Irving.

51

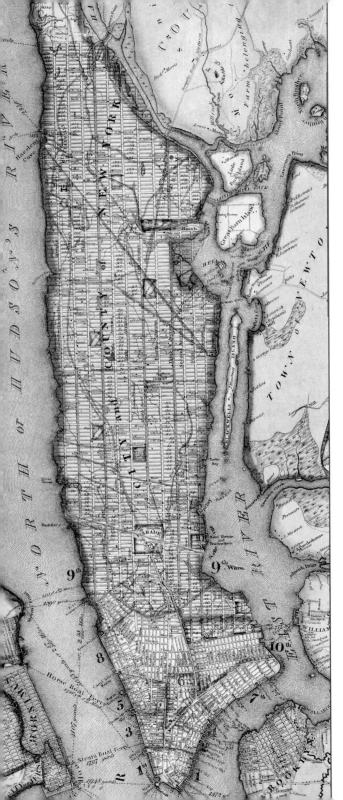

Tombs, a somber-looking 150-cell prison, was built on the site in the 1830s.

The Randel Plan

COMMERCE WAS booming and New York was growing rapidly. New theaters, hotels, shops, schools, and churches were built by the dozens as the 18th century became the 19th century. Parts of the East River and the Hudson River continued to be filled in to create more land, but to really grow, New York had to expand northward.

As settlement continued north, into Greenwich Village and toward 14th Street, there was no plan; streets were laid out haphazardly. On the west side, Washington, Greenwich, and Hudson Streets ran parallel to the Hudson River, while on the east side, Water Street, Cherry Street, Lombardy Street, Banker Street, and Henry Street were parallel to the East River, nearly 90 degrees different from the west side streets. The city government felt that something had to be done to regulate the city's physical growth. If there was no official plan, streets would continue to be laid out haphazardly, making travel and commerce more difficult.

◀ **An 1821 map of Manhattan showing the Randel Plan.**

The Randel grid system was created between 1807 and 1811 by engineer John Randel Jr. and was approved in 1817. Randel was part of a three-man commission in charge of planning for the city's expansion. The commissioners wanted a right-angle system: "A city is to be composed principally of the habitations of men, and strait sided, and right angled houses are the easiest to build." Randel began to make his survey, but angry property owners had him arrested several times "for trespass and damage committed by my workmen, in passing over grounds, cutting off branches of trees, etc." Finally, the commissioners received special authorization from the legislature to enter private property and cut down trees as necessary.

The grid began at Houston Street and stopped at 155th Street—who'd ever live *that* far north?—and made provisions for a parade ground from 23rd to 34th Streets between Third and Seventh Avenues. Look at a map of Manhattan and you'll notice that Broadway and Greenwich Village were spared from the plan. The Village was only spared west of Sixth Avenue because some streets were already being laid out and plots of land sold. A booklet of protest written anonymously by Clement Clarke Moore, author of the famous poem "'Twas the Night Before Christmas," helped the Village become an exception to the rule. The new grid meeting the old Village streets caused some curious complications, such as the crossing of 10th and 11th Streets by Fourth Street.

By 1828, development on Broadway only extended as far north as 10th Street. Old mansions, farmhouses, and estates north of that point were gradually parceled into individual lots and sold off. Those estates that didn't change hands were momentarily passed by the growing city. Streets were laid out around them, leaving these old structures "stranded."

In 1860, a solitary house on Second Avenue just north of 42nd Street sat atop a hill that comprised exactly one block in the grid plan. This house (and hundreds of others like it), along with its hill, would be flattened and the land developed in years to come. Stately country homes were demolished to make way for

The Buck Horn Tavern at what is now 22nd Street and Broadway, 1812. The grid plan eliminated the rural appearance of the northern parts of the city.

Randel Plan Game

SINCE ITS creation, the Randel Plan of 1811 has often been criticized as being too boring and uniform. People have accused it of destroying the city's natural character and geography.

In truth, laying out a city isn't easy. If it were up to you, what would you have done? Is there a better layout for the city? One of the big concerns in urban planning is the ease of getting from one place to another. In this activity, you will try your hand at being an urban planner and laying out New York City.

What You Need

✦ Plastic colored curling ribbon, at least 30 feet (from a party store)
✦ Rug or floor with plenty of space
✦ Different color curling ribbon, at least 200 feet
✦ Scissors
✦ Tape measure
✦ Toy car
✦ Green construction paper

The time is 1811. John Randel Jr. is selected to serve on a commission to map out the city's streets, but he becomes ill and they pick *you*

instead. Now the fate of the city's streets is in your hands!

Before trying to draw it out on a piece of paper, you'll need to experiment on a larger scale. Lay the 30-foot ribbon on the floor or ground in an elongated Manhattan shape that is at least 10 feet long and 5 feet wide.

Now cut the long ribbon into 10 strips that are 10 feet long and 20 strips that are 5 feet long (or other sizes as needed). Either on a floor or outside on dirt, grass, or concrete, lay out the strips of ribbon and then attempt to navigate your car from one point to another at various extremes of the "map."

Use green construction paper to designate parks. What is the best balance between an attractive layout and an efficiently navigable city?

Washington Slept Here

The Morris-Jumel Mansion, near 160th Street, is the oldest house in Manhattan. It was built in 1765 by a British colonel, and General Washington used it as his headquarters during the fall of 1776. After the British took over New York, it was occupied by British and Hessian troops. On July 10, 1790, Washington returned to the mansion as president, dining there along with members of his cabinet, including Thomas Jefferson, John Adams, and Alexander Hamilton.

The French emigrant Stephen Jumel and his wife Eliza eventually owned the house, and after Stephen died in 1832, Eliza remarried—to an elderly Aaron Burr, the former vice president. In 1903, the City of New York bought and preserved the property.

The Council Chamber at the Morris-Jumel Mansion.

Cornelius "Commodore" Vanderbilt in later years.

row houses, which were then demolished to make way for commercial low-rise buildings, which were in turn eventually demolished to make way for skyscrapers.

The Steamship and the Rise of Cornelius Vanderbilt

ONE OF the people present at John Fitch's steamboat demonstration at the Collect Pond in 1796 was New York politician Robert Livingston. Having seen the great potential of steam power, Livingston enlisted inventor Robert Fulton to devise a steam-powered passenger boat that could chug up and down the Hudson River.

On August 17, 1807, the ship was ready for a trial run to Albany. The *Clermont* stood at a dock on Barclay Street, as an anxious crowd waited, ready for a big disappointment. Instead, the ship's engines rumbled to life, and then it departed at an impressive speed of four miles per hour. So enthusiastic was Livingston that he made sure a law was passed giving Fulton a monopoly on steamship travel up the Hudson.

Other entrepreneurs did not think this law was very fair. A man named Thomas Gibbons had a steamship called the *Bellona*. In 1817, he hired Cornelius Vanderbilt (1794–1877) as his captain. When the *Bellona* docked in New York, police tried to arrest Vanderbilt for violating the steamship law. But Vanderbilt outfoxed them. He taught a woman how to steer the boat, and as it neared the New York docks, he would turn it over to her and disappear behind a secret panel in his cabin, silently waiting as the officers searched the boat.

The struggle over the rights to ply the Hudson went through the New York state court system. Finally, in 1824, the US Supreme Court heard the *Gibbons v. Ogden* case and decided that no state could grant an exclusive right of navigation on any of the principal rivers of the country. Navigation on the Hudson was finally free to all.

Vanderbilt worked hard and quickly became prosperous. At the height of his steamship career, Vanderbilt owned 66 ships, before moving on to a wildly successful career in railroads. He was worth $9,000 in 1817 and $75 million at his death 60 years later.

The Erie Canal

NEW YORK's merchants and shipping magnates suffered in 1807, after President Jefferson ordered American cargo ships to stay in their ports and forbade the shipment of cargo on foreign vessels. There were again difficulties when a fleet of British ships blockaded New York harbor during the War of 1812.

But things would soon improve. The construction of the Erie Canal between 1817 and 1825 was a huge boost to commerce in New York. Connecting the Hudson River to Lake Erie, the canal allowed easy transport of goods to and from the west. News of the canal's opening was transmitted in 81 minutes over a distance of 550 miles, from Buffalo to Sandy Hook, by the successive firing of a line of cannons 10 miles apart. Governor De Witt Clinton (1769–1828) and other dignitaries made the trip along the canal and down to New York's harbor, where Clinton emptied a keg of Lake Erie water into the ocean.

Around the same time, *packet ships* (ships that followed a scheduled route, carrying both cargo and passengers) began a regular weekly service from New York to England, making the trip in anywhere from 15 to 23 days. These packet ships were sailing vessels built for speed in the days before steam technology.

By 1840, *clipper ships* (high-speed ships with more sails than regular ships) were sailing from New York to California and even China. The firm of Howland & Howland owned more than a dozen packet ships and did heavy trade with South America. It sent ships to Peru and Chile laden with all manner of goods: crockery, ironware, steel, provisions, salt, barrels of brandy, wine, fireworks, gunpowder, muskets, lead, and silk shawls.

As time passed, ships grew faster. In 1860, the *Dreadnought* made it from New York to Ireland in just 9 days, 17 hours, and in 1864,

the clipper *Adelaide* beat the steamer *Sidon* to Liverpool.

Yellow Fever and Cholera

JOHN BARD, a leading doctor of the time, wrote in 1789 that New York was "one of the healthiest cities of the continent." However, New York was in fact a breeding ground for disease. As the settlement moved north, it got closer to the marshy and stagnant areas near present-day Chambers Street.

Chatham Square in 1812.

In 1791, an outbreak of *yellow fever* (a disease spread by mosquitoes) killed 200 people in the city. In 1796, an even more widespread outbreak occurred, killing 730, of which 600 were recently arrived foreigners. In 1798, yellow fever appeared beginning in August and killed 2,086 people in the city, and in 1803 another 600 or so died from the disease. In 1805, another 270 died; upward of 26,000 people moved from the interior parts of the city and from the streets near the waterside. The New York City Board of Health was created in 1805 to help deal with the outbreaks.

As the yellow fever outbreaks began to subside, a new and even more deadly disease made its appearance in the city: *cholera*, a result of waste in the streets and contaminated drinking water. Over 3,500 people died as a result of a cholera outbreak in 1832, and another 5,000 people in 1849.

Greenwich Village

GREENWICH VILLAGE, on the west side of Manhattan just below 14th Street, was known as Sappokanican by the Native Americans, and *Bossen Bouwerie* (Farm in the Woods) by the Dutch in 1633, when Governor Van Twiller established a tobacco plantation there. It was known for its pleasant, rural location away from the bustle of the city. It received the name of Greenwich in the early 18th century.

In 1816, a stage line was established between Greenwich Village and New York City, two miles to the south. The biggest factor in its growth was its place as an escape from the deadly outbreaks of illness in the city to the south. Mr. Marcelus, pastor of a church there, said he saw corn growing at the corner of Fourth and Hammond (11th) Streets on a Saturday morning, and the following Monday on that spot there was a boarding house capable of holding 300 people. Brooklyn ferryboats now made the trip daily.

New York in the midst of a yellow fever or cholera outbreak was a town under siege. From morning until night, anxious people hurried through the streets and a steady stream of carts laden with boxes proceeded toward Greenwich Village. Temporary stores and offices were quickly built, and in just a few days' time the Custom House, the post office, banks, insurance offices, and newspaper publishers relocated to Greenwich, which they believed was free from danger.

The Village temporarily became the center of New York's business. Once it was determined that the epidemic was over, people rushed to return to the city. A parade of carts and wagons rolled south, carrying merchandise and household furniture back to the stores

The Washington Square Arch (1892) is a Greenwich Village landmark.

and houses from which they had been taken several weeks before.

Greenwich Village soon became a permanent home to many new residents, including a host of artists and writers. The first person of note to live there was Edgar Allen Poe (1809–1849). He would be followed by Herman Melville, Mark Twain, and Edna St. Vincent Millay, who at one point lived in the narrowest house in the city, which was just 9½ feet wide.

Fashions of 1842, as printed in the *Ladies' Companion*, New York.

The Great Fire of 1835

AT AROUND 9 PM on the cold night of December 16, 1835, a patrolman discovered a fire in a warehouse at Exchange and Pearl Streets. A fire company arrived on the scene, but the fierce wind had spread the fire to 50 nearby buildings within 20 minutes. Firemen were forced to cut holes in the East River ice to obtain water, which soon froze in the hoses.

Philip Hone, former mayor of the city, kept a diary for many years. He recorded the events of the Great Fire of 1835:

The night was intensely cold, which was one cause of the unprecedented progress of the flames, for the water froze in the hydrants, and the engines and their hose could not be worked without great difficulty. . . . The fire originated in the store of Comstock & Adams, in Merchant street,—a narrow, crooked street, filled with high stores . . . occupied by dry-goods and hardware merchants. . . . When I arrived at the spot the scene exceeded all description; the progress of the flames, like flashes of lightning, communicated in every direction, and a few minutes sufficed to level the lofty edifices on every side. It crossed the block to Pearl Street. I perceived that the store of my son was in danger, and made . . . my way . . . to the spot. We succeeded in getting out the stock of valuable dry goods, but they were put in the square, and in the course of the night our labours were rendered unavailing, for the fire reached and destroyed them, with a great part of all which were saved from the neighbouring stores; this part of Pearl Street consisted of dry-goods stores, with stocks of immense value, of which little or nothing was saved. At this period the flames were unmanageable, and the crowd, including the firemen, appeared to look on with the apathy of despair, and the destruction continued until it reached Coenties Slip, in that direction, and Wall Street down to the river, including all South Street and Water Street; while to the west, Exchange Street . . . William Street, Beaver and Stone Streets, were destroyed. The splendid edifice erected a few years ago . . . known as the Merchants' Exchange . . . took fire in the rear, and is now a heap of ruins. The facade and magnificent marble columns fronting on Wall Street are all that remain of this noble building, and resemble the ruins of an ancient temple rather than the new and beautiful resort of the merchants. When the dome of this edifice fell in, the sight was awfully grand.

The Great Fire of 1835 destroyed the last vestiges of Dutch New York.

Every insurance company in the city went bankrupt after the fire, which destroyed almost 700 buildings, including the last surviving Dutch-era structures in the city.

Be a New York Journalist

Now it's your turn to try your hand at being a New York journalist or diarist like Philip Hone. The difference between a journalist and a diarist is simply that a journalist is expected to be more objective and straightforward in telling the story.

Watch or listen to the news from New York (or your own town) and pick a current event, or pick an event from New York's history, and write an article or journal entry as if you were there to witness it. If you pick a historical event, research it in a library or on the Internet to get more details. Use facts, and use your imagination to pretend you're there!

The Croton Water System

As the city's population grew, obtaining clean drinking water was more and more of a problem. A public well had been dug near Bowling Green by 1658, and more wells were dug at other locations shortly after, but they became contaminated. Water was obtained further north, at the "Tea-water Pump" located near Chatham Square.

In the 1770s, an engineer proposed to pump water from wells and the Collect Pond and send it through pipes to a reservoir at Broadway and White Street, but the Revolution prevented this scheme from going anywhere.

The Manhattan Water Company, founded in 1799 by Aaron Burr, represented the city's first water supply system. Burr's company built an iron water tank near the Collect Pond and pumped from a well using two 18-horsepower steam engines. It built a reservoir at Chambers Street and ran 20 miles of pipes (hollowed-out logs) from there to various parts of the city, supplying 1,400 customers with 700,000 gallons of water per day. It was a start, but clearly not a permanent solution for a city that required much more water than that.

In 1830, an elevated water tank with a 230,000-gallon capacity was built near a well at Broadway and 13th Street. The well shaft went 112 feet deep, and by 1833, seven miles of cast iron pipes from the water tower were laid.

In 1832, Colonel De Witt Clinton was hired to study the city's options for a reliable water supply. Clinton's report showed just how expensive it was for New Yorkers to get their water from springs and from sources in Long Island and New Jersey. He believed that the Croton River, north of the city, could supply 20 million gallons of water a day using gravity flow. He also recommended that a dam be built to channel this water into an aqueduct leading to New York.

Construction of this giant project began in 1837. A horseshoe-shaped aqueduct was built along the banks of the Croton River to the Hudson, then along the Hudson to Yonkers, then along the ridge between the Hudson and East Rivers, where it crossed the Harlem River on a bridge. This 1,450-foot-long stone "High Bridge" spans the river 140 feet above the water. Comprised of 15 semicircular arches, the bridge still stands today. From High Bridge, the aqueduct followed 10th Avenue to 108th Street, crossing eastward to a receiving reservoir.

The work was complete enough by June 1842 that a test could be performed to see if the water flowed properly from the Croton Dam to the Yorkville Reservoir. A specially prepared little boat, the *Croton Maid*, was placed in the water at the Croton Dam, and the next day it arrived at the Harlem River by power of the gravity flow. A few days later, the boat and its accompanying water were let into the Yorkville Reservoir in the presence of the governor and mayor as a 38-gun salute was fired. A huge celebration, attended by 180,000 cheering people, was held on the official opening day, October 14, 1842. The day began with a 100-gun salute at sunrise, followed by the ringing of the bells of all the churches, and then a grand parade from the Battery to City Hall Park.

The huge distribution reservoir, at Fifth Avenue between 40th and 42nd Streets, was the final destination of the Croton water before it was distributed to individual customers. The reservoir was one of the most talked-about sights in New York and featured a promenade around its perimeter that was a popular spot for an afternoon or evening stroll. Before the surrounding area was built up, the 50-foot-high walkway commanded a beautiful view of the surrounding area, and one could even see the hills of Westchester.

The Chambers Street Reservoir.

Crystal Palace and Latting Tower

By the 1840s, New York's status as a commerce capital was cemented. Wall Street was abuzz with activity every day. When the city was chosen to host the 1853 World Exhibition, it was confirmation of New York's standing in the world.

In 1852, construction was begun on a "Crystal Palace" at 40th Street between Fifth and Sixth Avenues. Made of 1,800 tons of iron and 15,000 panes of seven-inch-thick glass, the Crystal Palace was 365 feet long by 365 feet wide, capped by a magnificent dome.

President Franklin Pierce attended the opening day on July 14, 1853. Over 5,000 exhibitors from 25 countries and 30 states were represented. Exhibits included inventions of the day, such as the Colt revolver, the Morse telegraph, and McCormick's reaper.

Though the exhibition had attracted 1.25 million visitors by the time it closed in November 1854, it still lost money. The supposedly fireproof Crystal Palace was destroyed by flames in just 30 minutes in October 1858. In 1871, the site became Reservoir Park, and in 1884 it received its current name of Bryant Park.

On 43rd Street, opposite the Crystal Palace and built at the same time, was the 350-foot-high Latting Tower, the tallest man-made structure in the country. From the top one could see a distance of up to 60 miles. Designed by Warren Latting, the tower was an octagon, 75 feet wide at the base, built of wood and iron. There was a refreshment room immediately above the first story, and there were three observation decks, the first two served by steam-powered elevators. The highest deck was 300 feet from the base, and at each platform there were telescopes and maps of the

Crystal Palace (center) and Latting Tower (far left) under construction, 1853.

surrounding area. This venture was also a disappointment, and the tower was destroyed by fire in August 1856.

Five Points

THE FIVE Points was a notorious slum at what was then Cross, Anthony, Little Water, and Mulberry Streets, located on the still-somewhat-sinking site of what had been the Collect Pond. The inhabitants were mainly Irish, along with some Germans.

By the 1830s, the neighborhood was well known for its crime, violence, gangs, poverty, and disease. An 1854 book cited "miserable looking buildings, liquor stores innumerable, neglected children by scores, playing in rags and dirt, squalid looking women, brutal men with black eyes and disfigured faces, proclaiming drunken brawls and fearful violence." An 1869 account mentioned the "muck, and mire, and slime, reeking, rotting, oozing out at every pore of the pestiferous place."

Some of the neighborhood's most troublesome residents organized themselves into a violent gang called the Dead Rabbits. The 2002 film *Gangs of New York* was about the Five Points and the Dead Rabbits. The most notorious building in the Five Points was the Old Brewery, which was exactly that—an old

brewery that had been fitted out for apartments. This large building housed up to 1,200 people at one time.

The Five Points in 1827.

Oddities and Curiosities

NEW YORKERS have always loved museums filled with oddities and curiosities. In 1789, "Dr. King" arrived in the city with a collection of exotic animals to show, including orangutans, a sloth, baboon, monkey, buffalo,

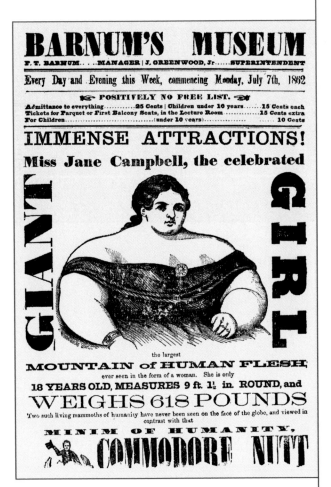

A Barnum Museum handbill from 1862.

porcupine, crocodile, swordfish, snakes, and birds.

Scudder's American Museum, located on Chambers Street in the former almshouse, featured an "Extraordinary and Grand Exhibition of Wonders of Nature and Art." The museum invited a ventriloquist and entertainer named Monsieur Saubert, trained in "Mimical Illusion and Magical Displays," for a special performance opening in the museum's New Saloon in 1834.

The showman Phineas T. Barnum saw potential in Scudder's and bought its contents for $15,000 in 1841, moved it to Broadway and Ann Street, and ran it for 25 years. Barnum's American Museum contained everything from historical artifacts to freaks of nature and wax statues, including a scale model of Niagara Falls (for which he paid $200), a so-called Feejee Mermaid, and whales in a saltwater tank in the museum's basement. In 1842, he introduced the 25-inch-tall, 16-pound Charles Stratton (Barnum renamed him General Tom Thumb), whom he paid $3 per week plus boarding for him and his parents.

To advertise, Barnum paid someone a dollar a day and gave him five bricks. He was to lay four of them a block apart—one on the corner of Broadway and Ann Street, another close by the museum, a third on the corner of Broadway and Vesey Street, and a fourth on the sidewalk in front of St. Paul's Chapel. Then, with the fifth brick in hand, he quickly walked from one to the next, at every point exchanging his brick with the one lying there without a word to anyone. Within an hour, the sidewalk was packed with people watching this strange ritual, many of them curious enough to follow the bricklayer into the museum.

The humorous Barnum had a sign at the back of his museum that read THIS WAY TO THE EGRESS. The curious customer, thinking an "egress" was some mythical creature, went through the doorway—but "egress" just means "exit." The customer found himself outside and had to pay 10 cents to get back in!

The museum was destroyed by fire in 1865. No people were killed, but Barnum's great white whale lay dead on the street, the glass of its tank having been shattered by the fire's heat.

The Eden Musee on West 23rd Street, which opened in 1884, was the first hall in New York devoted exclusively to wax figures. Exhibits included an organ grinder and monkey, a pencil vendor, a bootblack (shoe-shine boy), a tiger hunt, a scene from the Battle of Gettysburg, the Czar of Russia, President McKinley, the King of Denmark, Queen Victoria, the Emperor of Germany, the Sultan of Turkey, Pope Leo XIII, Beethoven, Christopher Columbus, and Theodore Roosevelt. After viewing the rest of the museum, one could pass into the Chamber of Horrors, featuring scenes of torture and executions, which was said in one review to be "too horrible for people with weak nerves." One visitor wrote, "Every day a wax figure is taken for a live man, and live people are mistaken for wax. I took hold of a waxen hand in one corner of the winter garden to see if the ring was a real diamond, and it flew up and took me across the ear in such a lifelike manner that my ear is still hot and there is a roaring in my head that sounds very disagreeable, indeed."

Castle Garden

CASTLE CLINTON, located at the southern tip of Manhattan at Battery Park, was originally intended to serve as a fortification during the War of 1812. It never saw military action, and in 1845 it was converted into a concert hall and renamed Castle Garden. The first performers were a band of Ethiopian singers and an Irish comedian. Other early Castle Garden performers were the Havana Opera Company and a tightrope walker named John Cline.

In September 1850, Castle Garden was graced by the presence of a famous singer, the "Swedish nightingale" Jenny Lind, who was brought to America by her manager, P. T. Bar-

Castle Garden in 1850.

num. Ever a showman, Barnum did a good job of drumming up interest before her arrival. He offered a $200 prize to whoever composed the best ode, "Greeting to America," to be sung by Jenny Lind at her first concert.

Thirty thousand people stood on nearby piers, streets, and rooftops awaiting Lind's arrival as her boat docked at Canal Street. Lind could barely get into the carriage waiting to take her to her hotel. Police had to fight back the masses of people. As the carriage wheels began to roll, the crowd deluged it with flowers. Thousands gathered outside her hotel and she had to make several appearances at the window to please the crowd. Two hundred musicians even came to the hotel to offer her a musical salute.

Tickets for the first performance were auctioned and a fee was charged to all who attended the sale, yet 3,000 people were curious enough to pay for the privilege, even though many could not actually afford to buy tickets. Though Lind's engagement was to last for many weeks, 4,500 tickets were sold just for the first performance. Five hundred people crowded the Hudson River in boats, aiming to somehow get into Castle Garden from the rear. Lind asked that her proceeds from the first two performances—about $10,000—be donated to local charities. Barnum guaranteed her at least $1,000 per show. After her 150 performances at Castle Garden, she was more famous than ever.

In 1855, Castle Garden was taken over by the city and became the Castle Garden emigrant landing depot, the precursor to Ellis Island, until 1890. From 1896 to 1941, it housed the New York Aquarium. It is now known as the Castle Clinton National Monument. A new aquarium opened in Coney Island, Brooklyn, in 1957.

Jenny Lind.

6

Innocence Lost

As New York City grew during the 19th century, it experienced some turmoil. Crime increased, and unrest, riots, and scandals plagued the city from the late 1840s to the late 1860s, as New York's population increased by half a million people in just 20 years. These growing pains were difficult to endure, but in the end, New York emerged stronger than ever.

The Astor Place Riot

TRAGEDIES ARE usually put on in theaters, but in one case, tragedy was caused by theater. The well-known American actor Edwin Forrest was friends with William Charles Macready, a popular English actor who had first appeared in New York in 1826. On Macready's 1843 American visit, a rivalry sprang up between the two actors, spurred on by the newspapers.

Who was the better actor? The rivalry became so bitter that when Forrest went to London in 1845, he was hissed so badly by the audience that he had to quit his engagement after only a few performances. Forrest next sought out Macready, who was then performing in Edinburgh, Scotland. Forrest hissed Macready at a sensitive moment in the play. Again the newspapers seized on this. When Macready visited America in 1848, a vicious war of words broke out between the two men, appearing in print in various newspapers.

On May 7, 1849, Macready began an engagement at the Astor Place Opera House. The theater was packed with his enemies, and he was booed from the stage. However, his friends convinced him to reappear on May 16. A crowd of Macready supporters was allowed into the theater, but there were still a good number of his enemies inside. Meanwhile, outside, Forrest's angry supporters had gathered. Inside the theater, the situation soon became too dangerous for Macready to continue, and he hurried out through a back door wearing a friend's cloak, barely escaping with his life.

The mob outside rioted and set forth to destroy the theater. The Seventh Regiment was called in, and the rioters fought with the soldiers. A total of 25 people were killed and more than 150 soldiers and 70 of the mob were injured in the chaos.

The Astor Place Riot.

The Dead Rabbits Riot

When the city's police force became corrupt in the 1850s, Mayor Fernando Wood (1812–1881) was blamed. The state legislature passed a law creating a state-run Metropolitan Police force that would include Queens, Brooklyn, Westchester, and Manhattan. Mayor Wood fought the law, but in May 1857, the State Supreme Court upheld it.

When the mayor refused to disband the Municipal Police force, his arrest was ordered. The Metropolitan force showed up at City Hall and tried to arrest the mayor, but they arrived to find him backed by a force of 300 Municipals. Fighting broke out and spilled into the street. Fifty-five policemen were injured. The mayor was arrested but was freed on bail and allowed to return to City Hall.

The feuding continued, and two separate police forces patrolled the streets of New York. The case next went to the appeals court, which upheld the law. Mayor Wood finally pulled his police from the streets, leaving only the Metropolitan Police.

The Dead Rabbits gang saw this turmoil within the city's police force as an opportunity to cause mayhem, and on the night of July 3, 1857, the gang attacked Metropolitan Police who were patrolling in the Bowery, but they were driven back by a rival gang called the Bowery Boys. The next day there was another clash between the police and the Bowery Boys in the Five Points. Women got involved as well, throwing bricks and pots at the police from the rooftops. On the ground, police and gang members clashed with sticks, stones, knives, guns, and bare fists. The military was called in to restore peace, but by the time they arrived all was quiet. Eleven people were killed and 50 wounded in the violence.

That wasn't even the worst 1857 had to offer. A financial panic in August led to almost 40,000 city workers being unemployed by winter.

The Dead Rabbits Riot, Bayard Street, July 1857.

Draft Riots

Rioters destroy the Colored Orphan Asylum, 1863.

WHEN THE Civil War began in 1861, tens of thousands of New Yorkers gladly volunteered to fight. Despite this, by 1863 the Union was in need of more troops. President Lincoln instituted a military draft with the Conscription Act, which had a clause stating that one could buy one's way out of the draft for $300. New Yorkers were not pleased with the idea of "the rich man's money against the poor man's blood." There were rumblings of a coming riot, but nothing happened on July 11, the day the Conscription Lottery began.

But on the morning of Monday, July 13, a mob formed at the conscription office at Third Avenue and 46th Street, drove out the enrolling officers, and set the building on fire. The police came but were quickly repelled. The mob robbed stores, tore down and desecrated American flags, and pillaged and burned the Colored Orphan Asylum building (Fifth Avenue and 44th Street). The mob of 5,000 then headed toward another conscription office on Broadway near 28th Street. They destroyed the conscription office, looted most of the stores nearby, then started on a march toward Mulberry Street, shouting, "Kill the police! Kill the police!"

Sergeant Daniel Carpenter assembled 200 policemen and ordered, "Hit for their heads, men, and hit hard." It took only a few minutes to dispose of the mob, and soon Broadway was cleared of all except the rioters who lay around the street with battered and broken heads. That evening the mob reformed and attempted to burn the Tribune Building on Park Row, but they were met by 100 policemen armed with revolvers. Thirty rioters lay dead in the street as a result.

By Tuesday morning riots had broken out in a dozen parts of the city, and although the police could check the mob at any one place, the whole force could not stop all the violence around the city. Small bands of rioters were roaming the streets, murdering every African American they encountered. Larger bands looted shops and burned houses. Mayor George Opdyke's house was badly damaged, and the residence of Henry J. Raymond, editor of the *New York Times*, was destroyed.

The rioting continued on the morning of July 15, but by afternoon troops of the Seventh Regiment began to arrive from Pennsylvania. Thankfully, it didn't take them long to restore order. The riots were a costly lesson to New York City. More than $2 million of property had been destroyed and hundreds of people lay dead.

Lincoln's Death

FOUR YEARS of Civil War was draining for New York. Over 50,000 of the state's soldiers were killed. When the war finally ended in the spring of 1865, the citizens of New York experienced a sense of relief, but their rejoicing was stained by deep sorrow at the loss of President Abraham Lincoln's life. News of Lincoln's assassination reached New York City at about 7 AM on April 15, 1865, instantly blanketing the city in grief. From that time until after the president's funeral, business in the city was suspended.

Funeral services were held at the White House on April 19. The body was then taken to the Capitol Building, where it lay in state until the 21st, when a funeral train set out for Illinois, stopping in New York City on the way. Lincoln's body was brought to the rotunda in City Hall amid the chanting of 800 singers and placed on a superb catafalque (platform). Church bells tolled, and City Hall Park was packed with mourners. Over the course of

Lincoln's funeral procession marches down Broadway, April 25, 1865.

Good Booth/Bad Booth

The Booth Theatre on 45th Street is named after Edwin Booth, brother of Lincoln's assassin, John Wilkes Booth. Like his infamous brother, Edwin Booth was also an actor. In 1869, he opened a theater at Sixth Avenue and 23rd Street.

The current Booth Theatre, which opened in 1913, was named in Booth's honor by the producer Winthrop Ames.

the next 24 hours, thousands of people waited in a long line to pass through and pay their last respects

On April 25, Lincoln's body was escorted to the railroad station by a procession nearly five miles in length, consisting of about 15,000 soldiers. In the afternoon, thousands of citizens gathered at Union Square to listen to a funeral oration by George Bancroft and a eulogy by William Cullen Bryant.

The Tweed Ring

WILLIAM MARCY Tweed (1823–1878) started out like any other ambitious New York politician, rising quickly through the ranks of local politics. A fireman at first, he began his political career at the age of 27 as a city alderman and was then elected to congress. He eventually became the leader of Tammany Hall, the New York Democratic powerhouse.

At the time, the new courthouse at 52 Chambers Street was already under construction. It became known as the "Tweed Courthouse," for good reason. It was nearly completed, with more than $4 million already spent, when Tweed and his pals came along and discovered that the building needed extensive "repairs." The original plasterwork in the building cost $531,594. The Tweed Ring submitted bills for $1,294,684 for "repairs to plasterwork." The original carpentry cost $1,439,619; "repairing" it before the building was finished cost another $750,071. For carpets, shades, and curtains, $675,534 was paid. For furniture, $1,575,782. Incredibly, the cost of the building increased by more than $8 million dollars; $41,190 was "spent" just on brooms! Tweed accomplished this mischief with the help of unscrupulous

The Tweed Courthouse.

contractors who marked up prices and submitted phony bills.

The courthouse wasn't Tweed's only moneymaker. He had inside information about the city's plans for widening Broadway. He and his friends knew exactly where and when work was to be done, and they quickly bought up land along Broadway in what became known as the "Front Lots Scheme." They bought a large plot near 42nd Street for $300,000 and

Nast's best-known Tweed cartoon.

were paid $700,000 by the city for a strip of that land on the street side, just a fraction of the overall plot. Tweed's cronies bought another lot for $24,000, were paid $25,000 for the strip that was seized by the city, and were left with a property that was then worth $35,000 because of the improvements. In all, for the widening of Broadway from 32nd Street to 59th Street, the city paid out $3 million to Tweed and his partners in crime before even putting a shovel to the ground.

Despite Tweed's attempts to seem kind (such as donating $50,000 to the poor people of his ward on Christmas Day 1870), New Yorkers were losing patience. Critical cartoons drawn by Thomas Nast and published in *Harper's Weekly* magazine didn't help. Tweed was so angry at these vicious (but true) cartoons that he forbade the Board of Education from ordering any textbooks published by Harper and Company, the magazine's publisher. *Harper's* didn't give in, and Nast's attacks continued.

Meanwhile, the former sheriff of New York, James O'Brien, who'd had a falling out with the Tweed ring, gave a *New York Times* reporter an envelope containing direct evidence of Tweed's criminal activities. Tweed and his pals were now frightened. They offered the newspaper's publisher $5 million not to publish the information, but he refused to be bribed. On July 8, 1871, the *Times* began to publish the details, and the public learned how much the Tweed ring had cost the city. Now Nast published one of his most powerful cartoons, showing members of the Tweed ring in a circle, each one pointing at the next, with a caption that read "Who stole the people's money?"

On October 26, 1871, Tweed was arrested. He was freed on bail and reelected to the state senate in the November election. In December, Tweed was indicted for fraud and felony. He was later convicted and sentenced to 12 years in prison and fined $12,000. He served 19 months and was then released on a legal technicality. By now the city had filed $6 million in civil lawsuits to recover the stolen money, and Tweed was quickly rearrested and held on $3 million bail. Since even he could not come up with that amount of cash, he went to jail.

Tweed was allowed visits outside of jail, and on one of these he escaped, was smuggled aboard a schooner, and reached Florida. From there he went to Cuba on a fishing boat but was arrested when he landed because the Cuban officers recognized him from Nast's famous cartoons. He managed to get away again and fled to Spain. He was again arrested, and in November 1876 he was brought back to New York. This time he went to jail for good, where he died on April 12, 1878.

Draw a Political Cartoon

POLITICAL CARTOONS are editorials— opinions—about current events, people in power, and the policies they make. These cartoons are usually both critical and funny at the same time. They use sarcasm or exaggeration, both in the drawing and in the caption, to make a point.

Thomas Nast's political cartoons helped bring down Boss Tweed in 1871. Imagine you are a cartoonist for a newspaper of the time, trying to show the public how Boss Tweed was bilking the city out of money with his Front Lots Scheme.

What You Need
✦ Paper
✦ Pen

Remember the key facts here. Tweed knew about the plans to expand Broadway before anyone else. He bought up properties, forcing the city to pay him for the strip of land it needed for the expansion.

In political cartoons, famous people or places might be represented by animals, things, or ordinary people. For example, a man in a used car lot saying "I spent too much" to his wife might represent a politician, and the clunker car he bought might represent a project he funded.

Come up with a few different ideas and sketch them out. Then you can tackle present-day politics. Have a look in the editorial section of your local newspaper for some examples of modern political cartoons.

DURING THE mid-19th century, Fifth Avenue became synonymous with class, style, and the best of New York, taking that title from Broadway. Once the wealthy began to build their mansions on Fifth, and with the construction of Central Park, its reputation as a fashionable locale (with no noisy elevated trains rumbling overhead) grew.

With an adult's permission or accompaniment, begin your tour at 59th Street, in front of New York's most well known hotel, the Plaza. Built in 1907 with an addition in 1921, the Plaza has hosted many celebrities over the years, from the Beatles to Theodore Roosevelt to Frank Lloyd Wright and F. Scott Fitzgerald. It is also the setting for the Eloise series of children's books.

Walk south on Fifth to 56th Street. At 725 Fifth you'll see Trump Tower (1983), built by developer and TV star Donald Trump—the location where *The Apprentice* is filmed. Have a look inside at the impressive six-story atrium with waterfall.

Next, walk to 54th Street and on the west side of the street you'll see the University Club (1899) designed by McKim, Mead & White. At the corner of 53rd Street is St. Thomas Church (1914), a French Gothic masterpiece.

Walk south to 51st Street, where you'll see on the east side St. Patrick's Cathedral (1879) and on the west side the *Atlas* statue (1937) and the massive Rockefeller Center complex (1930s), built on the former site of Columbia University.

The New York Yacht Club headquarters (1899), off Fifth at 37 West 44th Street, has an interesting sailing-related facade. At 7 West 43rd Street is the Century Association building (1891, McKim, Mead & White), another fine example of the wealth of the city.

Between 40th and 42nd Streets is the New York Public Library (1911), which was built on the site of the old distributing reservoir. Visit the third-floor Reading Room for an awe-inspiring sight.

If you're not too tired, make your way down to 34th Street. This intersection has been one of the most important in the city for 150 years, beginning with the construction of A. T. Stewart's mansion in the 1860s. William Astor demolished his mansion on Fifth Avenue and 33rd Street and built the Waldorf Hotel in 1893. Shortly after, his cousin John Jacob Astor demolished his mansion and built the Astoria Hotel next door. The two were combined into the Waldorf-Astoria in 1897. The hotel was demolished in 1929 to make way for the Empire State Building.

Opening of the New York Public Library, 1911.

A City of Contrasts

NEW YORK CITY in the second half of the 19th century was a city of great contrasts. Some neighborhoods were crumbling and poverty-stricken, while others were fantastically luxurious. Some parts of New York were bustling, while others were still practically rural.

In 1871, the railroad tycoon Cornelius Vanderbilt had Grand Central Depot built on 42nd Street between Lexington and Madison Avenues. West of the station were the Wellington Hotel and fashionable row houses. But much of 42nd Street east of Lexington Avenue was undeveloped, owned by an old lady named Mrs. White who sold goat milk and kept a large herd of goats that wandered around the neighborhood and napped on the steps of the neighboring Hospital for the Ruptured and Crippled. All around the city, new was meeting old and rich was meeting poor.

Immigrants and Tenements

As INDUSTRY, wealth, and the prestige of the city increased, so too did poverty and despair. With each passing year, more and more immigrants arrived in New York to seek their fortune. The annual rate of immigration to the United States quadrupled between 1844 and 1850. A potato blight in Ireland caused Irish immigration to soar in the late 1840s, and poverty and strife in Germany caused German immigration to spike between 1852 and 1854.

Overall, more than 5 million immigrants landed at Castle Garden between 1855 and 1890. The end of the Civil War, combined with increasingly poor conditions for peasants across Europe, created huge tides of immigration. What these people thought would be a better life than what they were leaving behind was sometimes better, but often worse. New immigrant families experienced prejudice from those who had been in New York for generations.

Between 1840 and 1870, the city's population tripled from about 300,000 to more than 900,000. The desirable parts of the city in the center of the island were off limits to poor immigrants, who were housed in *tenements* (multifamily dwellings) built on the less desirable land closer to the East River and Hudson River.

Families of 8 and 10 crowded into bug- and rat-infested apartments that would be a squeeze for even three people. Whatever plumbing was to be had was most likely shared by the people on that floor, including violent drunks, petty thieves, and those sick with contagious diseases.

These earliest of tenements were dark and dirty, and offered conditions that were breeding grounds for cholera, smallpox, and typhus. This led reformers to pass the Tenement House Act of 1867, which promoted more light and air. It said that tenements could cover up to 78 percent of a plot, that there had to be a 10-foot rear yard, and that there had to be air shafts or an open court area equal to 12 percent of the lot size. The Board of Health ordered the cutting of 46,000 windows in interior rooms in 1869. By then, the area of the worst, most dilapidated and foul slums had shifted northward along the East Side from the Five Points and Delancey Street to the stretch of land between 4th and 11th Streets and Avenues A and B.

In response to the tenement law, the layout of the newer tenement apartments changed

European emigrants boarding a ship bound for New York.

and evolved by 1879 into an I-shape. This gave all rooms a window or access to an air vent, and limited the number of apartments per floor to four. The result was far from perfect, though, since most rooms wound up facing the ventilation shaft, which was likely to stink from the garbage that was thrown down it by tenants.

One survey during the early 1890s found 1,400 people (300 families) living in just one block downtown. On the Lower East Side the population density was 300,000 per square mile, twice the density of the worst parts of London. Most tenements were built on 25-foot-by-100-foot lots, were five or six stories high, and could house up to 100 people. A city missionary wrote in 1892, "The sun never shines in the bedrooms of three-quarters of the people of New York City.... The suffering in July and August is often intense. The bedrooms become unbearable, and the roofs, fire escapes, and empty wagons are used as sleeping places.... There are scores of horrible, pestilential rat-holes which are utterly unfit for human habitation."

By 1891, about two-thirds of New York's population lived in 37,358 tenements, where rents ranged from $1 a month and up. Tene-

Tenement house on Laight Street.

BETWEEN 1892 and 1924, 22 million immigrants passed through the Ellis Island immigration complex, and many of them decided to remain in New York City. Ellis Island was opened to handle a growing volume of immigrants that was proving too much for Castle Garden.

Though there were other ports of arrival along the East Coast, chances are good that if your family immigrated to the United States during this period, at least one of your ancestors passed through New York City at some point. In this activity you will learn how to use online and other resources to trace your immigrant ancestors.

What You Need
✦ Family members to question
✦ Computer with Internet access
✦ Pen and paper

Get as much information as possible from your parents, grandparents, great-uncles and great-aunts, or anyone who might know the names of your immigrant ancestors. The Municipal Archives on Chambers Street has both indexes and actual records (on microfilm) for New York City vital records (years vary by borough before consolidation in 1898): Births 1847–1909, Marriages 1864–1937, and Deaths 1812–1948. In addition, every state has its own vital record collections that you can use depending on where your family comes from.

First check the vital record indexes available online at www.italiangen.org or www.germangenealogygroup.com. These sites are constantly adding new data, so check back every few months. About a quarter of births before 1910 weren't reported, because births often took place at home and the doctor or midwife neglected to officially report them. Once you have certificate numbers for your ancestors, you can visit the Municipal Archives to view (and get copies of) the actual certificate.

To find your ancestor's arrival at Ellis Island (which opened in 1892), go to www.ellisisland.org and perform a search. Once you find potential candidates, you can click the link to view each ship's register. Also available at www.italiangen.org are indexes to naturalization records from the 1860s to the 1950s. Once you find your ancestor and get the correct reference number, you can order a copy of the actual naturalization certificate from the National Archives.

Stevemorse.org has many great search tools, including one-step passenger arrival, naturalization, vital, and cemetery records. The information you obtain through that site can lead you to more detailed information elsewhere.

Census records are another valuable tool. Ancestry.com offers a free search, but you need a subscription to see the actual census pages. Censuses can tell you who your ancestors lived with and how many people lived in their building, as well as the country of origin of the people's parents, their occupation, and their age. Ancestry and similar sites also offer World War I and World War II Draft Registration Cards, which provide useful information about the people listed, as well as their signatures.

If your family arrived in the United States more recently, there are many resources to help you trace your ancestors in their country of origin. Try www.familysearch.org to view the available records in your family's homeland.

Inspection of immigrants at Ellis Island, 1911.

ment dwellers were constantly on the move, trying to find less-offensive lodgings.

The Danish American reporter Jacob Riis called attention to the plight of the tenement dwellers with his books *How the Other Half Lives: Studies Among the Tenements of New York* (1890), *The Battle with the Slum* (1902), and *Children of the Tenements* (1903). A new tenement law enacted in 1902 helped improve tenement conditions a bit more.

Street Vendors

NINETEENTH-CENTURY New Yorkers bought groceries from markets around the city and household supplies from drugstores or dry-goods stores. But they could also buy a wide variety of goods from street vendors. Those who couldn't afford to open a shop sold their goods around the city from pushcarts or buckets or even their pockets. These vendors usually lived in the slums and worked long hours on the streets, counting their profits in pennies, not dollars. Many of them were women and children trying to help support their families.

One of the most common sights in old New York was the corn vendor. From midsummer to late in the autumn, they roamed the streets selling hot corn from a pail, with accessories of a paintbrush and containers of butter and salt. Their piercing cries were designed to get your attention. One might call out, "Here's your nice hot corn, smoking hot, smoking hot, just from the pot! Oh what beauties I have got!" Another might yell, "Hot corn, hot corn!

Gum vendors on the Bowery, 1910.

Some for a penny and some two cents. Corn cost money and fire expense. Here's your lily-white hot corn!"

So common was this sight that one book published in 1854 was titled *Hot Corn: Life Scenes in New York*. The author told of coming across a 12-year-old girl selling corn at midnight. He told her to go home. She replied, "Oh, sir, my mother will whip me if I go home without selling all my corn. Oh, sir, do buy one ear, and then I shall have only two left, and I am sure she might let little Sis and me eat them, for I have not had anything to eat since morning, only one apple the man gave me, and part of one he threw away." The man bought all her remaining corn, and gave her extra money to buy herself a loaf of bread and some cakes.

Other street vendors carried trays containing baked pears soaked in molasses. There was also the "sand man"—barrooms, restaurants, and many of the kitchens in the city had sanded floors, and men in long white coats pushed carts filled with sand from Rockaway Beach in Queens. Other vendors offered to sharpen your scissors and knives, repair your locks or make keys, or sell you bundles of straw for filling beds, bundles of matches (sticks of cedar or pine soaked in brimstone), cylinders of lemon or mint candies, radishes, oranges, hot spiced gingerbread, spring water from Greenwich Village, brooms, fish, oysters, and clams. The clam man called out, "Here's clams, here's clams, here's clams to-day, they lately came from Rockaway—they're good to roast, they're good to fry, they're good to make a clam pot-pie."

Clam vendor on Mulberry Street, Little Italy, 1900.

Child Labor

BESIDES STREET vendors, there were about 100,000 children working in various factories around the city. Children from poor families were expected to help out in any way possible. By the early 1870s, there were an estimated 8,000 children working at envelope factories and thousands more working at gold-leaf factories, where they applied gold leaf to the edges of plates. Another 10,000 worked at paper-box factories, 8,000 at paper-collar factories, and 12,000 in artificial flower factories.

Thousands more worked in the twine factories, whose dangerous machinery resulted in many lost fingers and whose air was polluted by floating particles of cotton and flax. Also dangerous were the tobacco factories, where 10,000 children were engaged in preparing the tobacco. A magazine reporter taking a tour of a tobacco factory in 1873 saw a four-year-old boy stripping tobacco leaves for $1 a week!

The Children's Aid Society founded special night schools for those child laborers who after a day of hard work still wished to get an education. In addition to factory work, 19th-century kids had a wide range of other "professions"—almost anything imaginable, including working at barbershops and blacksmith shops, driving wagons, scraping paint,

Above: Seven-year-old Jerald Schaitberger selling newspapers at Columbus Circle, 1910.

Right: Sign seeking "small boys" to work at a button factory, 19th Street, 1916.

working in shoe stores, and serving as errand boys.

Eventually, child labor laws were enacted to protect young children and limit the hours worked by older children.

Mansions and Millionaires

BY CENTURY's close, the New York City area was home to nearly a third of the country's millionaires, who made their fortunes in many different ways—real estate, railroads, steel, coal, shipping. As the financial and social capital of the country, New York was the place to be. What better showcase for their wealth than the avenues of New York? The rich did not stay put. The most fashionable addresses moved further and further north as the city grew.

In the 1830s and '40s, Gramercy Park and Union Square were fashionable. By the 1850s, Fifth Avenue in the 30s was the spot. On the northeast corner of Fifth Avenue and 34th Street was the $3 million Italian marble mansion (1860s) of the department store millionaire Alexander T. Stewart, who arrived from Ireland in 1818 with little money and died one of the richest men in the world. On the southwest corner of 34th and Fifth Avenue was the William Astor mansion (built in 1857, demolished in 1893 and replaced with the Waldorf and Astoria hotels). The family ancestor, John Jacob Astor (1763–1848), was a German musical instrument maker who brought several of his instruments with him to America but met a furrier on the ship who advised him to trade his instruments for furs. He did this

and quickly saw the great potential of the fur industry. His original $500 investment in 1783 was $250,000 by the early 19th century and $25 million by the time of Astor's death in 1848.

These superrich residents spent money quite freely. George Jay Gould (1864–1923) had a chateau built on the corner of 67th Street and Fifth Avenue. When he was not satisfied with that one, he had it demolished in 1906 and had a new mansion built in a different style a few years later. In 1879, William Henry Vanderbilt and his son William K. Vanderbilt began a mansion at Fifth Avenue and 52nd Street. Over 100 workers were employed just to excavate the hole for the foundations. The double bronze doors were modeled after a famous set designed by the Italian Renaissance artist Ghiberti's "Gates of Paradise" at a cost of $25,000. In 1881, William Henry's other son Cornelius began a mansion at Fifth Avenue and 57th Street. William K. Vanderbilt held a costume Easter Ball at his mansion in 1883 at a cost of $50,000.

In 1902, industrial millionaire Andrew Carnegie's 64-room mansion was completed at the corner of Fifth Avenue and 91st Street (now the Cooper-Hewitt Museum). Directly across the street from Carnegie's home the German banker Otto Kahn had his mansion constructed. Finished in 1918, it was one of the

The Astor Mansion.

last great mansions to be built in New York. It was also one of the largest, with 80 rooms and quarters for up to 40 servants.

Dozens of exclusive clubs were formed during the late 19th century to cater to the rich, and some of their magnificent buildings still stand today; the University Club and the Harvard Club are two beautiful examples. J. Pierpont Morgan's mansion at Madison Avenue and 36th Street is one of only a few still standing today. In 1892, social advisor Ward McAllister coined the term "the 400"—a list of the top 400 society names, based on the number of people who could fit into Mrs. Astor's 35-foot-by-35-foot ballroom.

Department Stores

NEW YORKERS have always loved shopping. Alexander T. Stewart created the country's first department store, a four-story "Marble Palace" on the corner of Broadway and Chambers Street, in 1846. The store was unlike any other dry-goods store at the time. It was much larger and had a greater selection, and passersby could see the merchandise displayed through the large ground-floor windows. In 1862, he moved his store uptown to Broadway and 10th Street, in a building that became known as the "Iron Palace" (an example of the cast-iron facades that had been developed by James Bogardus in 1849 and were especially common in SoHo).

The area between 10th and 23rd Streets, along Fifth and Sixth Avenues, was for a while the department store headquarters of New York and became known as the "Ladies' Mile." Macy's, which would one day become the world's largest department store, was founded in 1857 by a former Nantucket whaling captain. The symbolic red Macy's star was actually a part of a tattoo on his arm. By 1877, the store occupied a series of 11 connected buildings at Sixth Avenue and 14th Street.

Hearn's (founded in 1879) was nearby, on 14th Street between Fifth and Sixth Avenues. At 18th Street was B. Altman and Company (1876). The six-story-high Siegel-Cooper & Company store was on Sixth Avenue between 18th and 19th Streets. A crowd of 150,000 attended the grand opening on September 12, 1896.

The city's shopping district later moved 20 blocks north, to Herald Square, where Macy's relocated in 1902 and the huge Gimbel's (1910) store was located until it closed in 1986. The Gimbel's building is now the Manhattan Mall (opened in 1989), home to several department stores over the years, including Abraham & Straus, Stern's, and most recently, J. C. Penney. Further uptown was Bloomingdales (first opened in 1872; located at 59th Street and Lexington Avenue since 1886). In 1930, Bloomingdales employed 3,000 people during peak seasons. One guidebook of the 1930s proclaimed that anything could be found in New York's department stores: "Even a monkey, an elephant, or a farm tractor can be supplied!" Department stores offered other things besides shopping; for many years, Macy's also held free cooking classes.

Competition for customers was fierce. During one 1919 price war over soap, Macy's and Hearn's kept slashing prices from the original eight cents per cake until the price was 24 cakes for a penny, and hundreds of customers were waiting in line for the unheard-of bargain!

Eating Out

IN THE early days of New York, there were no restaurants as we know them today. If you wanted a meal out, you could go to a tavern or an inn. Governor Kieft had the Stadt Huys (part tavern, part City Hall) built in the 1640s in part because he was tired of having to entertain visitors in his home. In 1676, there were four beer taverns and six wine taverns in the city. By 1892 there were 9,000 licensed saloons. One could have a drink and a meal at these establishments.

Originally a pastry shop that opened in 1827, Delmonico's was America's first fine dining restaurant. The original Delmonico's (on Wil-

Macy's opened its Herald Square store in 1902.

liam Street) was destroyed by the 1835 fire, and it reopened in 1837 on Broad Street as a full-service restaurant. The smart owners invited the editors of all the New York newspapers to a special preview night at the restaurant. The glowing reviews quickly helped cement the restaurant's place as a city landmark. When it reopened as a full-service restaurant in 1837, it had an 11-page menu, 27 beef dishes, 47 veal dishes, 20 lamb dishes, and 48 seafood dishes—everything from eel and turtle to rabbit and quail. The 100-foot-long wine cellar contained thousands of bottles of wine. Three famous dishes were coined there—eggs Benedict, lobster Newberg, and baked Alaska.

Restaurants for the common New Yorker became popular because with better transportation, people were commuting to work from a distance and couldn't go home for lunch, so having a place to eat during the day was important. Besides that, there were thousands of people who lived in furnished rooms with no kitchen. By the late 19th century, restaurants were common.

In 1891, you could get hash with bread and butter and coffee for 10 cents at a cheap restaurant. Some of the coffee stands offered a cup for one cent. Drugstores, five and dime stores, and department stores typically offered cheap food served quickly; you could get a cup of coffee for six cents and a complete meal for under 20 cents and be back at work before the lunch hour was over. The cheaper hotels offered a meal with wine for 35 cents. An 1891 meal at a restaurant such as Delmonico's cost at least three dollars.

By the 1890s, ethnic cuisine began to become more common as the flow of immigrants swelled. There were the Italian Riccadonna's at Union Square and Martinelli's on Fifth Avenue. Braguglias-Carreno, 13 Broadway, served Spanish dishes. Theodore Roosevelt, while city police commissioner, frequented a restaurant on Houston Street called Little Hungary. Lombardi's Pizza in Little Italy became the country's first pizzeria in 1905.

A new twist on restaurants opened in New York in 1912. Located in Times Square, the Horn and Hardart "Automat" restaurant featured a great variety of prepared lunch and dessert items behind an array of glass windows. You selected your item of choice and dropped coins in the slot, which would release the lock, allowing you to lift the door and take your item.

By 1939, there were 8,438 eateries around the city, representing the foods of 37 countries. The population has not really increased since the 1930s, but New Yorkers' desire to eat out has; as of 2010, there were 23,499 restaurants in the city. The average cost of dinner, including drink, tax, and tip, in 2010 was $41.17.

Though most of the old restaurants have come and gone, a few have remained open for over 100 years. Established in 1864, Pete's Tavern, at 18th Street and Irving Place, is the oldest continuously operating bar restaurant in the city. It is where the writer O. Henry wrote his famous story "The Gift of the Magi." One If by Land, Two If by Sea on Barrow Street is housed in what was once Aaron Burr's carriage house. Other historic bars include the Bridge Café (founded in 1794) and the Ear Inn (1817).

New York Lights Up

WE'RE SO used to New York's bright lights that it's hard to imagine a time when New York was lit by candles and flickering gas lamps. These lamps were first introduced to New York in 1825 along Broadway from the Battery to Canal Street. Attendants were needed to see that these streetlights functioned properly. By 1863, the New York Gas-Light Company (founded in 1823) had laid 130 miles of pipes under the streets, and the Manhattan Gas-Light Compa-

ny (founded in 1830) had laid 430 miles of pipes, lighting 30,000 street lamps and supplying gas to more than 50,000 stores and homes.

Thomas Edison (1847–1930) had invented the incandescent light bulb in 1879. But it wasn't so simple to introduce light bulbs into cities such as New York. Buildings had to be wired and fitted with these new bulbs, and a supply of electricity had to be available to power the lights. So in 1881, Thomas Edison bought two adjacent buildings on Pearl Street and had an electrical generating station built. Steam boilers were installed in the basement and six electrical generators were placed on the second floor. After much preparation, the station was finally ready and all the nearby buildings in the one-square-mile "First District" had been properly fitted.

On September 4, 1882, an engineer threw a switch at the Pearl Street Station, and Thomas Edison turned on the lights at an office building at 23 Wall Street, in the offices of the Drexel-Morgan Company. As the room became illuminated, Edison said, "I have accomplished all that I promised."

When first opened, the power station supplied electricity, exclusively for lights, for a total of 1,284 lights for 59 customers. Two years later, some offices were using electricity to power fans, and a few years after that, printing shops were using electric motors. New York was on its way to being fully illuminated by electricity, though the process took some time.

By 1892, the city still had 27,083 gas streetlamps and only 1,199 electric streetlamps. But developments such as electric lighting would prove necessary in coming years, when structural feats such as skyscrapers began to appear; just imagine how impractical it would be to have gas lighting in a 30-story building or an underground subway station. By 1914, Edison's New York company had 150,000 customers using more than 6 million electric lights.

Workers in New York City laying the underground tubes for electrical wiring.

The Brooklyn Bridge

THE EAST RIVER in the 19th century was one of the busiest stretches of water in the world. Though ferries had long been shuttling people between Manhattan and Brooklyn, a bridge was authorized in 1867 to better link the two cities.

The new bridge was designed by a German immigrant, John Augustus Roebling, a successful wire manufacturer and engineer who had begun building suspension bridges in Pennsylvania in the 1840s. His East River bridge was to have a total length of over a mile and a suspended span of 1,595 feet, capable of bearing a load of more than 18,000 tons. It would be the longest suspension bridge in the world and a major technological achievement.

Roebling died tragically in 1869, after an accident on a Brooklyn wharf that crushed his right foot. It was left to his 32-year-old son, Colonel Washington Augustus Roebling, to implement his father's design. Work began on January 2, 1870.

The first step in the construction involved the sinking of *caissons* into the riverbed to permit construction of the massive piers that would support the bridge. Caissons are like open-bottomed bells that are pushed down into the soil as the weight of the future foundation and tower is added on top. Excavation of the soil could then proceed inside the caisson, which was kept under pressure to prevent water and muck from leaking in.

It was a slow and tedious procedure and was hazardous for the workers underwater, who might suffer from *the bends* (when rapid depressurization releases nitrogen bubbles into body tissues). This condition struck Washington Roebling, who was left partially paralyzed. From that time on, he could only supervise the work from home, using a telescope to watch the progress from his window.

Once the foundations were laid, the anchorage towers were built, and the roadway had to be erected. Each of the cables suspending the roadway contained 5,000 wire strands of one-eighth-inch thickness. Imagine the wonder of the New Yorkers of the day who looked toward the river to watch the progress of this partly completed giant.

The bridge finally opened to much fanfare on May 24, 1883. President Chester Arthur and Governor Grover Cleveland were in attendance. The new bridge's towers rose to a height of 276 feet above the East River, dwarfing every other man-made structure on either side of the river. The bridge accommodated four carriageways,

The Brooklyn Bridge in an image drawn during the 1870s, before its completion.

a train, and an elevated pedestrian pathway that together transported close to 100,000 people per day. The bridge also contributed to the meteoric growth of Brooklyn, which by 1898 had almost a million inhabitants.

Many other bridges would follow. The Washington Bridge (1888) connected Manhattan and the Bronx. The Williamsburg Bridge (1903) and Manhattan Bridge (1909) connected Manhattan and Brooklyn, and the Queensboro Bridge (1909) connected Manhattan and Queens. The Hell Gate railroad bridge, spanning the Harlem River and crossing between Manhattan and Wards Island, was completed in 1916 and was the world's longest steel arch bridge.

St. Patrick's Cathedral

FOR MANY years, New York was primarily a Protestant settlement. The Catholic population of the entire state of New York was only 1,500 by the 1780s. There were no Catholic churches in New York until 1785, when St. Peter's on Barclay Street was built. By 1822, there were 20,000 Catholics in the city but only eight priests. By 1830, there were still only four Catholic churches in the city.

Poverty, hunger, and civil unrest in Europe, along with a growing impression that America really was the land of opportunity, helped contribute to the flood of Catholic immigrants into the country. The 1848 potato famine in Ireland caused a huge influx of Irish immigrants, most of them Roman Catholics. During the decades that followed, thousands of Germans, Poles, Italians, and other European Catholics came to New York every year.

Washington Bridge, seen here from the Bronx side, is the third-oldest bridge in New York. The oldest, High Bridge, is visible in the background of this 1916 photograph.

Some people felt threatened by the growing numbers of Catholics in the city. In 1844, a crowd of 1,000 athreatened to burn down St. Patrick's Cathedral, but Bishop John Hughes had 3,000 men at the scene to scare the rioters away.

The new St. Patrick's Cathedral was begun on August 15, 1858, at Fifth Avenue between 50th and 51st Streets. Construction was stopped for several years due to a lack of funding and the Civil War. The church finally opened in 1879 and is today one of the best-known churches in the world.

Bethesda Terrace in Central Park (72nd Street) in 1864.

Central Park

AT THE same time that the last remaining farms and open spaces in New York were rapidly vanishing, a beautiful park was being created out of one of the city's most unsightly areas. In 1851, Mayor Ambrose Kingsland asked the Board of Aldermen to look into creating a refuge in the city that would offer nature's amenities, a park that would provide both paths for Sunday carriage rides and outdoor recreation areas for the city's working class.

A rocky, overgrown, 700-acre plot in the center of Manhattan was chosen and purchased by the city in 1856. The area was increased to 843 acres (6 percent of Manhattan's current total acreage) in 1863 as the boundaries were extended to its present limits between 59th and 110th Streets and Fifth and Eighth Avenues.

Before the park was built, 59th Street was the dividing line between the most exclusive section of New York and one of the most run down. The chosen area was full of swamps and rocky outcroppings and was dotted with shanties occupied by about 1,600 people—Irish pig farmers, German gardeners, and Seneca Village, an established African American settlement with schools and churches of its own. Many Seneca residents had been landowners since before the Civil War.

The area had stagnant ponds and was overrun with animals. There were tens of thousands of wild dogs and cats, cows, pigs, goats, geese, and chickens roaming around. Some residents lived in halfway decent homes, others in huts made of wood scraps picked up near the river and sheets of tin, made by flattening cans.

An 1857 design competition for the new park was won by Frederick Law Olmsted (parks superintendent) and Calbert Vaux (a landscape architect). The winning plan was one of 33 submissions received. Called "Greensward," it aimed to create the illusion of a natural wilderness in the English romantic tradition.

Thousands of trees were planted, hills were created, water was imported to create lakes, and even boulders were moved and imported. More than 10 million cartloads of material and debris were brought into and out of the park during construction.

One impact of the park's success was a booming real estate market for nearby land. An 1869 advertisement offered an entire block between 9th and 10th Avenues and 63rd and 64th Streets: "Only 800 feet distant from Central Park, on high commanding ground, [this] is the most eligibly located property in that section of the city.... The terms of sale are such as to enable every one to secure a lot for a future home (while prices are yet low) in what must become in an incredibly short space of time the most fashionable and desirable quarter of the city."

The crowning achievement on the east side of the park was the completion of the Metropolitan Museum of Art in 1880, on Fifth Avenue between 80th and 85th Streets. This, along with the opening of the American Museum of Natural History on the west side of the park in 1877, helped attract other museums to the area in later years.

Over time, many enhancements were added to the park. A zoo was constructed in 1864, though it was not part of the original plan. The Wollman skating rink was added in 1949. Sadly, a freak snowstorm in October 2011 destroyed 1,000 of the roughly 24,000 trees in the park, including some of the oldest.

The American Museum of Natural History (opened in 1877) seen circa 1900.

The Obelisk

The 69-foot-high obelisk in Central Park at 82nd Street and Fifth Avenue, behind the Metropolitan Museum of Art, was a gift from Egypt to New York City in 1882. It was made in 1,600 BC and weighs 448,000 pounds. Originally erected at the Temple of the Sun at Heliopolis, Augustus Caesar had it removed to Alexandria in 12 BC. It cost $102,576 to transport to and erect in Central Park.

The obelisk in Central Park, circa 1903.

Put on a Broadway Show

IN THE 1890s, Arthur Conan Doyle, author of the Sherlock Holmes stories, wrote a one-act play called *Waterloo*. It debuted in London with Doyle's hero, Henry Irving, in the lead role. The play was produced in New York in 1899–1900 at the Knickerbocker Theatre (Broadway and 38th Street; in 1906 the theater was the first on Broadway to have a moving electrical sign), with Irving again in the lead role. On November 16, 1899, *Waterloo* was presented at the Broadway Theatre as part of the annual Actors Fund of America Benefit. In this activity, you'll put on a production of this play, specially adapted for your use.

What You Need
+ 4 cast members and a director
+ Stagehands to arrange the set
+ Computer with Internet access
+ Printer
+ 4 chairs and a table
+ A broom (to represent a gun)

Cast
+ Corporal Gregory Brewster, age 86
+ Sergeant Archie McDonald
+ Colonel James Midwinter
+ Nora Brewster (the corporal's grand-niece)

For the adapted transcript, refer to www.panchyk.com. Print out four copies of the play.

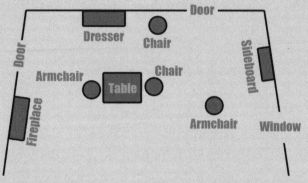

Set layout.

Look it over and assign the parts. You probably won't be able to memorize all the lines, so you can perform the play while holding the script.

The director should make sure the cast is following the stage directions and reading their lines properly. Most importantly, have fun, and try to imagine yourself performing before a turn-of-the-century New York crowd.

The Great White Way

THE MORE New York grew, the more the entertainment business boomed. The Park Theatre opened in 1798 on Park Row, and the area soon became the center of the theater scene. One of the most famous early theaters was the Bowery Theatre, which opened in 1826 on the bowery just below Canal Street and was destroyed by fire and rebuilt several times.

As the city expanded northward, so too did the theater district. By the mid-19th century, Union Square was the theatrical hot spot. The 14th Street Theater opened in 1866, with 1,600 seats. The Union-Square Theatre opened in 1871; the Academy of Music in 1854 at 14th and Irving Place; Irving Hall at 15th and Irving Place in 1860; and Steinway Hall (a concert hall) on 14th between Union Square and Irving Place in 1866.

By the last quarter of the century, theaters began to migrate farther north toward Longacre Square, renamed Times Square with the construction of the *New York Times* headquarters in 1905 at the intersection of Broadway and Seventh Avenue at 43rd Street. One of the first theaters in the Times Square area was the Broadway Theatre, which opened in 1887 at Seventh Avenue and 41st Street. In

1895, there were 40 theaters and opera houses in Manhattan, with total seating capacity of 62,000; 7 were located in the Times Square area, between 38th and 44th Streets, and 6 in the Union Square area.

The nickname "the Great White Way" was coined by a newspaper reporter in 1902, because of all the bright lights adorning the buildings and billboards, and the name stuck. According to one 1917 book, "It is a gaudy, garish region . . . the electric signs, with all their prodigal waste of light, are hideous to the eye, and they insult the soul with base advertisements. They leap the dome of heaven in letters of fire to proclaim the virtues of a Chewing Gum or a Breakfast Food." The gaudy lights became synonymous with Broadway, and to this day the theater district is known for its colorful flashing signs. Many of the beautiful theaters built in the early years of the 20th century are still in operation today.

Another thing for which Times Square is known is New Year's Eve. The first New Year's celebration at Times Square was in 1904, connected to the opening of the *New York Times* headquarters. These days, Times Square is host to hundreds of thousands of people every December 31 who count down the minutes and seconds to the new year and watch the huge "ball" drop.

Madison Square Garden

THE FIRST Madison Square Garden—originally called the Hippodrome—opened in 1873 in the abandoned passenger station of the New-York Central & Hudson River Railroad at Madison Avenue between 26th and 27th Streets.

In 1890, a new, gigantic Garden was built on the same site. The new building was 465 feet long by 200 feet wide and featured a tower that soared 332 feet high, making it one of the highest structures in New York. On its opening night of June 16, 1890, there were 17,000 people in attendance to watch an orchestra perform. It also had a café and a rooftop garden.

The most famous event to take place at the Garden wasn't a show, it was a murder; in 1906, the Garden's architect, Stanford White, was shot and killed on the rooftop by a jealous Pittsburgh millionaire named Harry Thaw, whose new wife, Evelyn Nesbit, had been friendly with White before her marriage to Thaw.

A third Madison Square Garden, no longer anywhere near Madison Square, opened on Eighth Avenue between 49th and 50th Streets in 1925 and hosted boxing, hockey, basketball, and circus events.

The fourth and current Garden opened at 32nd Street and Seventh Avenue in 1968 and

Broadway, circa 1905.

The 1890 Madison Square Garden was one of the city's tallest buildings.

is not only not near Madison Square, it is also round. It hosts the Knicks (basketball) and the Rangers (ice hockey), as well as concerts.

Statue of Liberty

THE STATUE of Liberty, which has graced New York harbor since 1886 and is one of the best-known symbols of New York City, was a gift from the people of France. The idea of a French-made monument to be erected in America as a memorial to independence and a celebration of the friendship of France and the United States was first mentioned at a dinner in 1865 by a French politician, writer, and admirer of America named Edouard-Rene Lefebvre de Laboulaye. One of the guests at that dinner was the sculptor Frederic Bartholdi (1834–1904), who was deeply moved by Laboulaye's words. A few years passed, and in 1871, Laboulaye again mentioned the idea, and told Bartholdi to go to America and propose this monument.

When Bartholdi returned to France he developed the design of what would become the Statue of Liberty, inspired by one of the seven wonders of the ancient world, the Colossus of Rhodes, which guarded its harbor. He had seen Bedloe's Island (now Liberty Island) during his trip and felt that its location in New York harbor

was ideal. The star-shaped old fortress—Fort Wood—could serve as a platform for the pedestal upon which the statue was to be placed.

Construction of the huge statue's pieces (copper sheathed over a steel framework) began in Paris in 1875. Money was raised by the French people to create the sculpture, and then by the American people to erect it. To celebrate the United States Centennial, Bar-

The Statue of Liberty in an 1884 drawing.

tholdi shipped the arm and torch to be exhibited at the 1876 Philadelphia Exposition. During the early 1880s, the torch was exhibited in Madison Square Park in Manhattan, and visitors could ascend to the observation platform and look out toward the site of its future home. It was then shipped back to Paris for completion.

The French frigate *Isere* arrived in the Lower Bay of New York on Wednesday, June 17, 1885, and two days later she was escorted by a large American squadron to Bedloe's Island, where the pieces of the statue were landed in 241 crates.

October 28, 1886, was dedication day, and the harbor was filled with boats as spectators watched the statue's unveiling from the Battery. President Grover Cleveland gave a speech on Bedloe's Island as the French flag draped over the statue was removed to reveal the finished Liberty. It was originally copper-colored, but in time it developed its familiar oxidized green color.

The statue, which portrays Liberty Illuminating the World, stands 305 feet high altogether, from the base of the stone-faced concrete pedestal to the tip of the copper torch. A 53-foot-deep concrete foundation firmly anchors the statue to the ground. Before the statue's centennial in 1986, it underwent a major $87 million rehabilitation.

Trolleys, Horsecars, and the El

TRANSPORTATION IN 19th-century New York was a mess—literally! With over 100,000 horses in the city, there was manure everywhere. And besides that, congested streets and no traffic lights meant traveling around the crowded city was slow.

An 1867 report said that "underground railways passing under streets present the only

The El tracks were double-decked along the Bowery from Chatham Square to Canal Street, as seen in an early-20th-century image.

The Blizzard of 1888

In March 1888, a mighty storm blew through New York, with wind gusts reaching 50 mph. A total of 21 inches of snow fell over three days, but the fierce wind caused incredible drifts of up to 20 feet in spots. The city was entirely shut down.

The storm closed the post office, the exchanges, and the banks, and snapped telephone and telegraph wires. Dozens of people died as a result. The East River was so thick with ice that people could walk across it to Brooklyn. Transportation was completely crippled, and all rail lines were stopped for days.

From the March 24, 1888, cover of *Harper's Weekly*, New York firemen struggle to answer an alarm during the blizzard.

speedy remedy for the present and prospective wants of the city of New York in the matter of the safe, rapid, and cheap transportation of person and property."

The early railroads in the city, built between 1831 and 1858, were horse-drawn cars that ran along tracks on Second, Third, Sixth, Eighth, and Ninth Avenues and along the Hudson River. These horsecars traveled on an infrequent schedule and competed with and were slowed by horse-drawn carriages as well as pedestrians. They were not a reliable or efficient means of transportation, especially once the city's population exploded after the Civil War.

The first elevated railway was built with carriages pulled by cables connected to a stationary underground steam engine. This was soon replaced with a steam locomotive pulling trains on a three-mile section that opened in 1870. The idea was so successful that construction of these elevated trains (Els, for short) proceeded very quickly.

As of 1895, there were 8- to 11-mile-long elevated rail lines along Second, Third, Sixth, and Ninth Avenues (and several more in Brooklyn). There were still also 45 other horsecar and trolley lines throughout Manhattan, and another 50 lines in Brooklyn. A city law stated that the rail lines had to run cars at least every 20 minutes between midnight and 5 AM.

By 1894, there were also 29 different ferries running between Manhattan and Brooklyn, Queens, and New Jersey. Ferries had been an important part of travel for hundreds of years. There were an astounding 133 different steamboat routes offered during various times of the year (some ran only during the summer) from New York City to New Jersey, upstate New York, and New England, with fares ranging from 10 cents to Fort Lee, New Jersey, to $4.00 for Martha's Vineyard. Most of the Hudson River routes sailed from docks around West 10th Street. Voyages to Long Island and New England began at Peck Slip or other nearby East River piers.

There were 12 rail bridges or footbridges over the Harlem River, connecting Manhattan and the Bronx. As the number of bridges crossing the East River increased over the next couple of decades, the ferry lines decreased in importance.

In time, the elevated railways were found to spoil the environment, with their noise, dark shadows on the streets below, and engines that spewed sooty smoke, oil, and ash, at least until they were electrified by 1899. All Els, except those in the outer boroughs, were eventually demolished and most were replaced by subways. The Ninth Avenue El was demolished just before World War II and the scrap was sold to the Japanese.

Then and Now Game

NEW **Y**ORK City has changed greatly over the years. There are very few places in the city that look anything like they did 200 years ago, but you might be surprised at what traces are left of turn-of-the-20th-century New York.

In this activity, you'll see for yourself the differences and similarities between New York circa 1900 and the city more than a century later.

Adult supervision required

What You Need

+ Digital camera
+ Computer with word processor
+ Pad of paper and pen
+ New York City guidebook (e.g., the *AIA Guide to NYC*)

On this page are four vintage photographs. Your mission is to head to each of these locations and take a photo from approximately the same vantage point and distance as the old pictures. All four locations are easily accessible via subway.

Take note of some of the interesting-looking buildings and write down their addresses. When you have captured the present-day scenes, upload the images to your computer. Included here are links to the vintage photographs on the Library of Congress site. You can download them and then lay out old next to new image in a word processing document.

+ www.loc.gov/pictures/item/det1994020586/PP/
+ www.loc.gov/pictures/item/det1994000531/PP/

+ www.loc.gov/pictures/resource/det.4a17017/
+ www.loc.gov/pictures/item/nyo360
  .photos.119925p/

Which buildings that were in the old photographs are still standing today? How have they changed? What other differences do you notice? (Examples: trees, signs, streets, sidewalks, people, vehicles, etc.) You can use your NYC guide and the Internet to research the buildings (using the addresses). Which of the four sites looks the most like it did 100 years ago, and which has changed the most?

Fifth Avenue looking north from 51st Street, circa 1905.

23rd Street, East from Sixth Avenue, 1908.

Fifth Avenue looking south from 25th Street, circa 1905.

Central Park West looking north from 72nd Street, 1890.

8

The City That Never Sleeps

As the 20th century approached, New York was a bustling modern city. The old reservoir at 42nd Street was demolished in 1899 to make way for a new public library. Also in 1899, the New York Zoological Park was opened in the Bronx, housing 1,000 animals. In the first seven weeks, despite especially bad weather, more than 100,000 visitors came. And most importantly, in 1898, the city annexed the outer four boroughs to become Greater New York and reach its present size.

Strong and Roosevelt

NEW YORK in the early 1890s was a corrupt mess. Though Tweed had come and gone, Tammany Hall remained all-powerful. Bribes and political arm-twisting were commonplace.

New Yorkers finally had enough, and in the fall of 1894 they elected Republican reform mayor Colonel William Strong (1827–1900). Strong made improvements to the city government, enforced stricter tenement laws, and created the Board of Education. The new mayor also appointed future president Theodore Roosevelt (1858–1919) as police commissioner.

As with the rest of city government, the police department was corrupt. Appointments to become a patrolman were not based on merit; they were purchased for $300. Newly minted patrolmen were eager to make up this money by extorting it out of liquor dealers, saloon owners, and street vendors.

One of Roosevelt's improvements was the introduction of a civil service examination and a reference check, which eliminated 80 percent of the candidates. He also changed the promotion system from a political game to a merit-based system. In one case, he made a sergeant out of a veteran patrolman who had rescued 25 people from drowning and had been cited by the US Congress for his bravery but had never been promoted because he lacked political backing.

Cartoon showing Mayor Strong as St. Patrick, driving out the corrupt Tammany snakes.

The Consolidation Act

THOUGH WE'RE quite used to the idea of five boroughs, for more than 250 years New York was Manhattan only. Parts of the Bronx—Morrisania, West Farms, and Kingsbridge—

Cruller Crackdown

In 1893–1894 alone, there were 4,300 tenement fires. One cause of tenement fires was the cruller (donut) bakery, which was often located in the basement of a tenement building. Crullers were usually made in the middle of the night, and if the fat in which they boiled spilled, a fierce grease fire began, endangering the sleeping tenement dwellers. Stricter laws under Mayor Strong resulted in 119 city bakeries giving up the cruller in 1896 rather than comply with the new fire safety regulations.

Draw a Gibson Girl

NEW YORK has long been a haven for artists. The renowned landscape painter Albert Bierstadt had a studio on 10th Street beginning in 1861. In the 1930s and '40s, New York was home to many abstract painters, such as Piet Mondrian (one of his best-known works is called *Broadway Boogie Woogie*), Mark Rothko, and Willem de Kooning. New York was also the center of the Pop Art movement in the 1950s and '60s, and Jasper Johns, Andy Warhol, Larry Rivers, and Roy Lichtenstein all had studios in the city.

In the 1890s, illustrator Charles Dana Gibson was among many illustrators in New York trying to sell their drawings to magazines and newspapers. Gibson caused a sensation with the introduction of a very pretty, distinct-looking young woman in his drawings. She soon became known as "the Gibson Girl," and at the height of her popularity her likeness was appearing on all kinds of items.

When asked how he came up with this uniquely American girl, Gibson said, "I saw the girl of that type in the streets, at the theaters, I saw her in the churches, I saw her everywhere and doing everything. I saw her idling on Fifth Avenue, and at work behind the counters of the stores. From hundreds, thousands, tens of thousands, I formed my ideal."

What You Need
+ Ultra-fine-point black felt-tip pen or roller-ball pen
+ Several sheets of tracing paper
+ Unlined white paper, at least 24 pound in weight
+ A model

Study the drawing on this page. Notice the characteristics, especially the use of very fine lines. Note the detailed way the hair is drawn, the simple beauty of the face, and the stylish clothes.

First practice drawing fine, curving strokes next to each other. Try duplicating the Gibson Girl's hair and other features separately, and then try to draw your own version of a Gibson Girl. You can draw from this or other images you find on the Internet, or use a friend as a model.

"BIG GAME"

Gibson Girl drawing called "Big Game."

were annexed in 1874. With only a narrow river separating Manhattan and the Bronx, it was easy to travel between the two places.

The idea of consolidating Staten Island, Brooklyn, Queens, and the rest of the Bronx with New York City first surfaced in 1890 but went through a series of debates and protests before a commission was created to draft a charter that would accomplish the incorporation of Greater New York.

A vote on consolidation was taken in November 1894. Manhattan residents voted 62 percent to 38 percent in favor of consolidation. In Brooklyn, it was nearly 50 percent to 50 percent. Queens and Staten Island were strongly pro-consolidation.

It became official on January 1, 1898, even after a veto by the mayors of Brooklyn and New York. The "new" New York was now 3.1 million people strong, up from 1.8 million, with an area of more than 350 square miles. Of the outlying boroughs, Brooklyn led in population with about 1 million people, followed by the Bronx (200,000), Queens (100,000), and Staten Island (60,000).

The coming of the subway to the outer boroughs meant that New Yorkers could own a private home in the outer boroughs and be at

Greater New York City as drawn in 1895.

work in Manhattan within 30 minutes to an hour. Thousands of identical private houses, many on 25-foot-by-100-foot lots, sprang up in the space of a few years. Along with them came brand-new elementary schools to serve the burgeoning population of children on what in some cases had still been farmland a few years earlier. But before long, these boroughs' populations would explode just as Manhattan's had. By the 1940s, Brooklyn, Queens, and the Bronx all surpassed the 1 million mark in population.

Coney Island

LONG BEFORE consolidation, New Yorkers were flocking to Coney Island in Brooklyn. This five-mile-long strip of sand along the Atlantic had long been a favorite bathing spot for locals, but once the huge 660-foot-long Manhattan Beach Hotel opened in 1877, followed by the Brighton Beach Hotel in 1878, greater crowds came.

Among the area's attractions were a 150-foot-high, elephant-shaped hotel/restaurant/dance hall, two 1,000-foot-long iron piers, concerts, and nightly fireworks. There were also amusement parks beginning in the 1890s, featuring rides and attractions. The most well-known ride, the Cyclone roller coaster, was built in 1927 and is still in operation today.

During its peak years, Coney Island had 10 million visitors annually. Further wonders were added after the turn of the century, making Coney Island more famous for its amusements than its beaches.

The *General Slocum* Fire

CHARTERED BY St. Mark's Church in the German neighborhood of the Lower East Side of Manhattan, the steamer *General Slocum* was to take 1,200 parishioners to a Sunday School picnic on Eaton's Neck, Long Island, on the morning of June 15, 1904. Besides the passengers, there were 23 crew members, about a dozen waiters, and some musicians on board. When the boat, built in 1891 and recently inspected, left its pier at Third Street and the East River, everything was fine.

Not long after that, a fire began on the ship. The flames spread rapidly, and the captain rushed to beach the vessel on the nearest available land: North Brother Island. But before he could reach it, hundreds of panicked passengers had jumped into the water. About 1,100 of the 1,300 on board died, either burned to death on the boat or drowned in the turbulent waters.

Though other boats tried to help, they could not get near enough to the *Slocum* until she had run aground. Several people were awarded medals of bravery by the United States Life-Saving Service, including a 15-year-old girl recovering from scarlet fever at a hospital on a nearby island who rescued nine children from the water.

This tragedy was so traumatic to the German Americans in the *Kleindeutschland* (Little Germany) neighborhood downtown (most of whom had lost someone in the disaster) that they moved uptown to Yorkville, a newer German community in the 80s between Second Avenue and the East River.

Newspaper headlines, 1904.

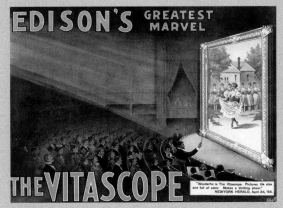

Be a Tin Pan Alley Songwriter

TWENTIETH-CENTURY NEW YORK was alive with music—all kinds of music. Many jazz musicians' careers, including those of the great Duke Ellington and singer Lena Horne, took off in Harlem at nightclubs like the Cotton Club. Meanwhile, downtown, some of the biggest Broadway hits and popular standards were being composed by the likes of George and Ira Gershwin and Irving Berlin.

Sheet music was big business in the days before the phonograph and radio really took off. People would buy the music to play on their pianos. New York music publishers and songwriters were scattered around the city, but beginning in the late 19th century several of them opened offices on West 28th Street, between Fifth and Sixth Avenues. The street became known as Tin Pan Alley, possibly because of the clanking sound of many of the piano hits of the day.

Many of the most famous composers of the time were published by Tin Pan Alley firms, including Scott Joplin, the Gershwins, and George M. Cohan. There is a plaque on the sidewalk of 28th Street commemorating the street's illustrious past. The music-publishing business soon moved further uptown, but the name stuck.

In this activity you will write and publish your own sheet music. Music publishers did not rely only on great and catchy tunes to sell music; they also relied on attractive cover art. Your challenge here is to compose catchy lyrics and design a good-looking cover. On this page you'll see two examples of New York sheet music covers.

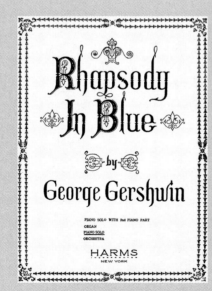

Rhapsody in Blue, 1927.

The Midnight Fire Alarm, 1900.

What You Need

✦ Set of colored magic markers, pencils, or paints

✦ Sheets of white paper, 8½ inches by 11 inches

✦ Digital camera

✦ Computer with photo-editing software

Come up with a title and write a song of your own. Hint: If you're stumped, pick an existing song you like!

Now look at the two examples of sheet music covers on this page. Try your hand at both a graphical cover—one that is mostly fancy lettering and designs—and one with an actual image. You can draw or paint an image, or you can photograph one (1930s sheet music covers often featured photos of the stars who sang the songs). Set a scene that relates to your song title and lyrics and have a couple of friends dress up and pose with some props. Then you can snap their picture.

Import the picture into a photo-editing program and "jazz" it up a little. Next, import the image into a word-processing document and type in the title at the top, your name at the bottom, and add a border!

The Subway

THE FIRST underground railway—the subway—in New York was a short, experimental run that went along Broadway from Warren Street to Murray Street. Alfred Beach, editor of *Scientific American*, constructed this subway with his own money. His original idea, patented in 1867, was to create an underground rail line to shuttle letters and packages around the city. He expanded on this to create a test run for passengers in 1870.

Beach used a special hydraulic shield to construct the tunnel without disturbing the street above. Inside was a pneumatic train in an eight-foot brick-lined tube; compressed air pushed it from one end of the tunnel to the other, a distance of 200 feet. In its first year, 400,000 passengers paid 25 cents each to ride this strange wonder.

Despite its popularity, the idea never went any further, and the subway tunnel was sealed in 1873. (It was rediscovered by workmen in 1912 during the construction of a subway along Broadway.) The idea of a subway system for New York was shelved until decades later; construction of the city's permanent subway system finally began on March 24, 1900.

The first subway opened on October 24, 1904, and ran from City Hall up the east side to Times Square, then up the west side to 145th Street. Construction took four years and cost $56 million. Workmen found little streams beneath the ground and, in one place uptown, a spring was found that, in the old days of New York, had formed a pond on the surface.

The subway route went directly under the statue of Columbus at Columbus Circle, which had to be supported until the tunnel under it was finished. Blasting had to be done to build

Alfred Beach's proposed Broadway subway, 1870.

the section through the rockiest hills in Upper Manhattan, above 157th Street. In spots, the subway tunnel is 200 feet below the surface. There weren't too many accidents during construction; the most serious was an explosion in the Park Avenue tunnel that broke all the windows in Grand Central Station and nearby buildings.

Subway construction, upper Lexington Avenue, 1912.

In the early days of the subway, the lines were operated by independent groups: the Interborough Rapid Transit Company (IRT) and the Brooklyn-Manhattan Transit Corporation (BMT). The Independent (IND) was the first city-owned line; it opened in 1932. Now New Yorkers could get almost anywhere in the city in a fraction of the time it would have taken before. And best of all, the streets above were a little less chaotic than they had been before.

The New York City Transit Authority was created in 1953 to take over all subway, bus, and streetcar operations. The Transit Authority was placed under the control of the state-level Metropolitan Transportation Authority in 1968.

Subway fare was 5 cents until 1948, 10 cents until 1953, when it rose to 15 cents, then 20 cents in 1966, 30 cents in 1970, 50 cents in 1975, 60 cents in 1980, and 75 cents in 1981. By 2009, the fare was $2.25. MetroCards were first introduced in 1993, and the subway token was discontinued in 2003.

Sweatshops and the Shirtwaist Fire

As THE city's population exploded, the market for cheap clothing increased dramatically. Immigrants were not only customers; they were also the manufacturers. New York soon became the country's leading clothing production center, and working conditions were usually horrendous, with 14-hour days and dangerous and filthy conditions. Seamstresses and piece workers were sometimes fined for imperfect work and made to pay for broken equipment. Many even ate and slept in the so-called sweatshops, in the same room where the work was done.

Besides tenement house sweatshops, there were larger factories in operation all around the city. In March 1911, a fire broke out in a fabric scrap bin at the Triangle Shirtwaist factory at Washington Place and Greene Street, on the top two floors of a 10-story building. A lack of fire escapes, locked interior doors, and crowded conditions on the factory floor caused 146 girls and women to lose their lives, some jumping out the windows to their death. A few days later, about 75,000 people took part in a demonstration march (which 500,000 people watched) demanding safer working conditions.

By the 1920s the Garment District was located primarily in the 30s between Seventh and Eighth Avenues. In 1938, 2,000 factories in New York City produced 77 percent of the country's women's clothing, 87 percent of its feathers and plumes, and 82 percent of the country's fur clothing.

Though the Garment District has shrunk and few clothes are made in New York any-

more, there are still plenty of fabric and sewing equipment stores in the West 30s. The television show *Project Runway* is filmed at the Parsons School of Design on Seventh Avenue and 40th Street, and the Fashion Institute of Technology (founded in 1944) on Seventh and 27th remains a popular college for future designers.

Women in an Elizabeth Street sweatshop, 1908.

Manufacturing City

UP UNTIL the mid-20th century, New York was a center for industry and manufacturing, not only of clothing but of all kinds of goods. Smokestacks could be seen in every direction.

In the 19th century, one of the most industrial areas of the city was alongside the 3.8-mile-long Newtown Creek in Brooklyn/Queens. There were over 50 refineries lining the creek, including oil refineries, fertilizer and glue factories, sawmills, lumberyards, and coal yards.

In the 1930s, New York produced 89 percent of the country's lapidary work (gemstone cutting and polishing), 63 percent of printed and published matter, 51 percent of all perfumes and cosmetics, 35 percent of the nation's musical instruments, 18 percent of the roasted coffee, and 11 percent of all the baked goods.

Factories were likely to be located along the East and Hudson Rivers in Manhattan, and then later along the waterfront in the outer boroughs. The six-story New-York Biscuit Company plant, at 10th Avenue between 15th and 16th Streets, was one of the largest buildings in the city, at 525 feet long and 206 feet wide. It had 40 ovens, could process 1,000 barrels of flour a day, and was the world's largest producer of crackers in the 1890s. The Ansonia Clock Company occupied an entire city block in Brooklyn and employed over 1,000 people. The Kreischer & Sons Brick Works occupied eight acres in Staten Island, and its kilns popped out 70,000 bricks per day.

As land values increased and neighborhoods became more residential, many of these factories closed down and moved production first to more rural areas and then overseas. The effect of all this industry was also dangerous, as waterways such as Newtown Creek were polluted with by-products of the manufacturing process.

Baseball in New York

BASEBALL, WHICH according to legend was invented in New York State in 1845, has been an important fixture in New York City since the mid-19th century. The first professional New York teams were the Giants (formed in 1883) and the Brooklyn team, the Superbas (formed in 1883), later called the Bridegrooms, the Trolley Dodgers, and the Dodgers. The Dodgers cemented a special place in history in 1947, when Jackie Robinson became the first black player in the major leagues.

The Giants were home to one of the greatest pitchers of all time. Hall of Famer Christy Mathewson (1880–1925) was a Giant for almost

The Kreischer & Sons Brick Works, Staten Island, 1890.

his entire career, from 1900 to 1916. In 1908, he won 37 games (a National League record). That year, the Giants were locked in a close race with the Chicago Cubs, and "Matty" pitched in 9 of the last 15 games to help his team. He won at least 22 games for 12 straight years, beginning in 1903, and finished his career with an amazing record of 373-188. He was one of the first five players inducted into the Baseball Hall of Fame. His teammate Rube Marquard won 73 games between 1911 and 1913. John McGraw was the Giants manager from 1902 to 1932, leading them to 10 National League pennants and three World Series championships.

The American League Yankees were originally called the Highlanders. The team originated in Baltimore in 1901 as the Orioles and moved to New York in 1903. The name Highlanders was supposedly due in part to the high ground upon which the team's baseball diamond was located (165th Street). The name "Yankees" was coined when one day a newspaper editor did not have room for "Highlanders" in a sports headline and used "Yankees" instead. The name caught on.

The Yankees moved to the newly built Yankee Stadium, along the Harlem River in the Bronx, in 1922. The most famous Yankee, Babe Ruth (1895–1948), arrived in 1920 from the Boston Red Sox. He was a pitcher with Boston, but switched to the outfield when he joined the Yanks. He would spend the rest of his career with the Yankees, playing alongside other legends such as Joe DiMaggio and Lou Gehrig. For many years, Ruth held the record for most career home runs (714).

In 1927, the Yankees played one of the best seasons in baseball history, with a record of 110 wins and only 44 losses. That was also the season that Ruth set the record for the most single-season home runs (60), which would stand for 34 years until another Yankee, Roger Maris,

The 1889 Brooklyn Bridegrooms.

Play Stickball

NEW YORK has been a baseball town for a long time. City kids loved the sport but rarely had the luxury of a real baseball field on which to play. *Stickball* and *stoopball* were popular games that New York City kids played during the mid-20th century—right on their own doorstep.

There are many varieties of these baseball-like games. Stoopball is played by throwing a ball against the front steps leading to one's house. One player faces the steps, while the other is in the street or across the street, trying to catch the ball. This game was very popular but is not very safe. In this activity, you'll try out a version of stickball.

What You Need
+ A parent or guardian
+ Wooden-handled broom
+ Roll of black electrical tape
+ Thick, colored chalk or bright-colored electrical tape
+ Blue racquetball, pink rubber ball ("spaldeen"), or tennis ball
+ A friend

Have your parent or guardian remove the bristles from a broom or cut off the tip of the broom end of the wood. Wrap the black tape around the stick, from one end to the other, leaving about 2 inches between the spirals. When you get to the end, crisscross the tape and spiral the other direction. Repeat this until the entire broom is covered in black tape. This prevents splinters and protects the wood from shattering.

Now find a stone or brick wall that you can use for your strike zone, such as a school building in a school yard or a tennis practice wall in a playground. Use the colored chalk or tape to outline a rectangular strike zone that is roughly 2 feet high by 1 foot wide and whose bottom is roughly at your knee level.

Take turns playing three three-out innings. The pitcher stands about 20 or 25 feet from the wall and pitches. Balls and strikes are counted as in regular baseball. A hit ball caught on the fly is out. A bounced ball is an out if the pitcher/fielder can throw it back into the strike zone after catching it. Make up foul lines and distance markers to designate doubles, triples, and home runs.

broke it. In 1930, Babe Ruth received the biggest contract in baseball history to that point, when he signed for two years and $160,000. Since their founding, the Yankees have won 27 World Series, more than any other team, thereby becoming the most loved and most hated and feared team in all of baseball.

The National League New York Metropolitans, or Mets, were formed in 1962 and first played at the old Polo Grounds in Manhattan before moving into the new Shea Stadium in Flushing, Queens, for the 1964 season. They started life as lovable losers, managed by the colorful baseball veteran Casey Stengel, finishing with a dismal record of 40 wins and 120 losses their first season and 51 wins and 111 losses their second year.

In 1969, the "Miracle Mets" surprised the sports world and finished with a 100–62 record and won the World Series. In the mid-1970s, the Yankees dominated baseball after a 12-year drought by making it to the World Series three years in a row, from 1976 to '78. In 1986, the Mets had a 108–54 record and won a World Series that featured one of the most shocking moments in baseball history: in game 6, Mookie Wilson's grounder rolled through the legs of Boston's Bill Buckner, allowing the Mets to win the game.

In 2000, the Yankees met the Mets in the World Series, nicknamed the "Subway Series," and won, four games to one. It was the first time since 1956, when the Yankees beat the Dodgers 4–3, that two New York teams faced each other in the World Series.

The Race for the Sky

UNTIL SEVERAL innovations at the end of the 19th century, the tallest objects in the city were church steeples. But then the use of structural steel frames allowed for much greater flexibility than stone or wood. Another factor was more efficient excavation techniques, which allowed the deep trenches necessary for tall building foundations. Instead of men digging trenches by hand, machines now did this excavation work much more efficiently. The invention of the elevator in the 1850s allowed people to be effortlessly carried to any floor, no matter how high. In the late 1880s the first true skyscrapers began to rise.

By 1894, the tallest building in the city was the American Surety Building, on Broadway at the corner of Pine Street. It was 23 stories and 306 feet tall. The 320-foot-high Empire Building, completed in 1898, had 25 floors serviced by 10 elevators and had space for a workforce of 2,200 people. The 300-foot-high, triangle-shaped Flatiron Building (1902), at Fifth Av-

enue and 23rd Street, is one of the city's most well-known and attractive skyscrapers.

Within a few years, the Singer Building (612 feet) and the Woolworth Building (792 feet) rose to amazing new heights. The Woolworth Building was the tallest building in the world for 17 years.

These new buildings were modern marvels. Many were like cities in themselves. One could mail a letter, have lunch, go to the bank, get one's shoes shined and hair cut, and buy candy, a newspaper, or flowers—all without leaving the building.

Between 1930 and 1940, even in the midst of the Depression, New York builders went ever higher. Thirteen of the city's tallest skyscrapers were completed between 1930 and 1932, including the Art Deco masterpiece Chrysler Building (the world's tallest building for a few months), the towering Empire State Building (the world's tallest building for decades), and the impressive Rockefeller Center complex.

Construction on the Empire State Building began in March 1930. It officially opened on May 1, 1931. The building has 6,500 windows, almost seven miles of elevator shafts, and required 60,000 tons of steel. The visibility on a clear day from the 102nd-floor observatory is 80 miles. While King Kong never actually

The Singer Building (demolished in 1968).

climbed the building as depicted in the 1933 classic film, a B-25 bomber did crash into the Empire State Building on a foggy morning in 1945, hitting between the 78th and 79th floors, killing 13 and injuring 25.

By 1939, there were 32 buildings 500 feet high or taller in the city. New York was the skyscraper capital of the world for many years. As of 1950, 18 of the 20 tallest buildings in the world were located in New York City.

New York skyline at night, 1914.

F. W. Woolworth and the Five and Dime

BORN IN upstate New York, Frank Winfield Woolworth (known as F.W.) was a discount store innovator. His idea was to take ordinary items that were slow sellers and promote them, offering them at a uniformly low price of five cents. The sign that read ANY ARTICLE ON THIS TABLE FIVE CENTS was a successful lure to customers.

Woolworth opened his first store in Pennsylvania in 1879, and his first store in New York City in 1894. By 1914, there were 742 Woolworth stores and 40,000 employees in the Woolworth empire. By this time, his stores sold 60 million pounds of candy and 8 million women's housedresses a year. In 1918, he sold a total of 54 million handkerchiefs. He was able to sell cheap by buying in bulk. By ordering 144,000 rings that normally sold for 50 cents, he was able to offer them for 10 cents apiece and still make a profit.

In 1915, Woolworth's earned an average of 9.9 cents for every dollar of goods sold. That may not seem like a lot, but all the nickels and dimes added up. Woolworth was a very rich man. His home on Fifth Avenue and 80th Street featured a $35,000 pipe organ, which he played himself.

The chain went out of business in 1997. There were plenty of other five and dime stores

Skyscraper Walking Tour

THE AREA surrounding and just south of City Hall Park contained some of the earliest and most spectacular New York skyscrapers. Ask an adult for permission or to accompany you on a tour. Start at the Municipal Building (1), completed in 1916. Designed by McKim, Mead & White, the elegant Municipal Building is 580 feet high and was the largest government building in the world when completed. A 30-foot-high statue called Miss Civic Pride graces the top.

Walk south from the Municipal Building to Park Row, on the east side of City Hall Park (also called Newspaper Row), to the former site of the World Building at Frankfort Street. After Joseph Pulitzer took over the *World* in the 1880s, circulation increased tenfold. He introduced photos and sensational stories to the front page. The World Building (2) was the tallest in the world, at 309 feet high, when completed at Pulitzer's direction in 1890. It was demolished in 1955 to make way for a Brooklyn Bridge ramp.

Though not so impressive now, the 13-story New York Times Building (3) (today owned by Pace University) at 41 Park Row was one of the tallest in the city when completed in 1889. Continue walking south. The 381-foot-high limestone Park Row Building at 15 Park Row (4) was the tallest in

the world from 1899 to 1908. At its completion it had 10 elevators, 2,080 windows, 1,770 doors, and 7,500 electric lights.

Walk south along Park Row until it meets Broadway. Continue south on Broadway. Look to the west, and you'll be able to see the newly built Freedom Tower (5), the tallest building in New York at 1,776 feet high, and the former site of the Twin Towers. Continue south on Broadway to Liberty Street. You are now at the former site of the Singer Building (6), once the world's tallest, which was demolished in 1968 and replaced with the 743-foot-high One Liberty Plaza, completed in 1973 (not even as tall as the Singer Building was!). Keep going south on Broadway, and on the east side of Cedar Street you will see the beautiful 38-story Equitable Building (7) at 120 Broadway, completed in 1915. As you continue south you will see Trinity Church (8), built in 1846. This was the city's tallest building for several decades, until the late 19th century.

Now double back north on Broadway to your next stop, the $13.5 million Woolworth Building (9). Located at 233 Broadway, the 792-foot-high Wool-

worth Building was paid for by the dime-store millionaire F. W. Woolworth himself, entirely in cash. Completed in 1913, the gothic masterpiece was termed the "cathedral of commerce." It was the tallest in the world for 17 years. Be sure to look closely at the detailed stonework!

Continue north on Broadway. At 256 Broadway you'll find one of the city's earliest skyscrapers, Home Life Insurance Building (10), completed in 1894, among the world's tallest when it was completed.

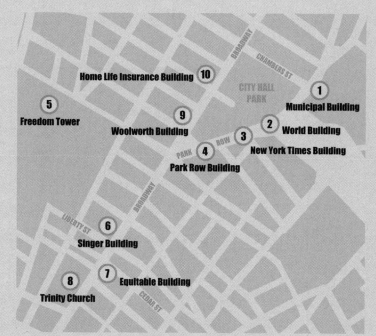

in New York, such as McCrory's, but Woolworth's was the biggest and most famous.

Prohibition

A GROWING anti-alcohol movement in the country led to the passage of the 18th Amendment to the US Constitution in 1919, which outlawed the sale or manufacture of alcohol.

Bars were closed, but that did not stop New Yorkers from indulging. *Bootleggers* (a name derived from smugglers' habit of keeping flasks of alcohol hidden in their boots) manufactured their own alcohol, and it was sold at secret bars that were often hidden in the basements of attached row houses. These so-called *speakeasies* also offered gambling and live entertainment. Admission was given by password or recognition through a peephole. There were a whopping 30,000 such establishments in the city during the 1920s. Bootlegging was big business, and it gave rise to notorious New York gangsters such as Dutch Schultz and Jack "Legs" Diamond.

There were plenty of agents employed to bust these illegal operations, the most famous being Izzy Smith and Moe Einstein. The heavyset pair wore comical disguises and gained the confidence of the bartender, then performed the bust. Their costumes included a Yiddish gravedigger, Russian fisherman, football player, German pickle packer, and Hungarian violinist. Between 1920 and 1925 they made a total of 4,392 arrests and confiscated 5 million bottles of liquor. With the passage of the 21st Amendment in 1933, which repealed the 18th Amendment, the speakeasy was history, and alcohol became legal again.

Agents Izzy and Moe share a toast at a New York City bar, 1935.

Wall Street Lays an Egg

NEW YORK has long been the nation's financial capital. By the 20th century, vast fortunes were being accumulated on Wall Street, on the trading floor of the New York Stock Exchange. The so-called Roaring '20s were very good to investors. Business was booming, stock prices soared, and the rich became richer.

And then, suddenly, it all came crashing down. All eyes were on Wall Street on October 29, 1929, as investors began to sell off. A panic ensued, and stock prices plummeted. Billions of invested dollars vanished in a heartbeat. The headline of *Variety* read WALL STREET LAYS AN EGG.

The crash had a domino effect on the entire American economy. Panicky people crowded the banks to withdraw their money, and many banks failed. Millions lost their jobs. New York was hit hard. Within two months, there were 6,000 people peddling apples on the street corners of the city. Soup kitchens and bread lines were common sights in the 1930s.

With America's entry into World War II in 1941, the economy picked up, as many thousands of New Yorkers got jobs in nearby defense plants building parts for airplanes and bombs.

Unemployed workers in front of a shack on East 12th Street, 1936.

World's Fairs

TWO OF the biggest attractions in city history were the World's Fairs (1939–40 and 1964–65), held at Flushing Meadow Park. About 500,000 people attended the opening day of the 1939 World's Fair, and a total of

45 million visited over the course of the fair, which featured hundreds of pavilions and exhibits from numerous different countries and states, as well as corporations demonstrating futuristic product prototypes.

Among the attractions were a "Tree of Life" carved from the trunk and branches of an elm planted in 1781 by Revolutionary War prisoners in Connecticut; 200 cows being milked daily on a revolving platform; an orange grove transplanted from Florida; the largest model railroad ever constructed; the largest opal in the world; a scale model of New York City so large that the Empire State Building was 23 feet tall; a singing fountain; a display of 1 million tulips; and a flight to Venus "so real you'll swear you've been there and met the folks."

Admission to more than 150 exhibit buildings was 75 cents for adults and 25 cents for children. The Unisphere (from the 1964 fair), is still standing today. It was the largest earth model ever built, at 140 feet high and weighing nearly 900,000 pounds.

Below: The Trylon and Perisphere at the 1939 World's Fair.

Right: A family looks out over the fairgrounds, circa 1940.

The Landmarks Commission

BY THE mid-20th century, New York's historic past was rapidly vanishing. No law prevented owners from demolishing and replacing a historic building. But the biggest blow came in 1963 with the destruction of Penn Station (1910). The owner decided to replace it with an underground station and an office building/new Madison Square Garden.

The New York City Landmarks Commission was founded in 1965 because of the public outcry over its loss. In 1968, Grand Central Station was saved from destruction when the lessee sought to gut the building. The Landmarks Commission vetoed the plan, and the fight went all the way to the US Supreme Court, which upheld the legality of New York's landmarks laws. The Singer Building, however, was not so lucky. It was demolished in 1968, having not received landmark status.

The city's preservation track record has improved greatly since the 1960s. South Street Seaport was an ambitious project of the 1970s and '80s that took several blocks of dilapidated buildings along the East River waterfront and not only restored them but also created a tourist destination. The most notable group of buildings, a series of four-story brick warehouses called Schermerhorn Row, after the original owner, date to about 1812. The South

Street Seaport Historic District covers several blocks and three piers.

One preservation effort that predates the Landmarks Commission is Historic Richmondtown, founded on Staten Island in the 1930s by the local historical society. Numerous endangered old buildings from around Staten Island were moved to the site and preserved as a museum.

The original Penn Station was demolished in 1963.

119

Make New York Bagels

THERE ARE many theories on the origin of the bagel, but the facts that can be agreed upon are that bagels trace their history as far back as 17th-century Poland. Bagels were a staple of Eastern European Jews, and when hundreds of thousands of them immigrated to New York in the 1880s, they settled in the Lower East Side of Manhattan and brought their bagel recipes with them. By 1900, there were 70 bakeries on the Lower East Side. Bagels could be stacked on a dowel, through that iconic hole in the middle, and sold by street vendors. Bagels soon became a city favorite.

Most New Yorkers will tell you that the city's bagels are the only "real" bagels. Some say it's the New York City water; maybe it's just years of secret recipes shared among members of the Bagel Bakers Union, founded in Manhattan in 1907.

It's generally agreed that bagels are special because they are first boiled or steamed, which brings out a shiny surface after they are baked. They have a crisp crust and a soft, chewy interior. Recipe variations include mixing whole wheat flour with white; adding baking soda, lye, honey, or barley malt syrup to the boiling water; adding toppings such as sesame or poppy seeds before baking; and varying the baking temperature, from 350 to 600 degrees.

Nothing beats a fresh bagel hot out of the oven. Try making your own with this recipe.

Adult supervision required

What You Need
+ 2 cups warm water
+ 2 tablespoons active dry yeast
+ ¼ cup vegetable oil, plus extra for bowl
+ 1 tablespoon salt
+ 1 teaspoon and 2 tablespoons brown sugar (separated)
+ 5 cups or more all-purpose flour
+ 4 quarts water

Dissolve the yeast in the warm water. Add the oil, salt, and 1 teaspoon of brown sugar. Gradually mix in the flour until a stiff dough forms. Knead for 10 minutes on a floured surface, adding additional flour as needed until the dough is elastic, not stiff.

Grease a large bowl with oil. Place the dough in the bowl, turning it over to coat in oil. Cover and let rise in a warm place until doubled in size, about 1 hour. Punch down and knead the dough for 2–3 minutes. Divide into 18 pieces and roll each into a rope, 6 inches long and 1 inch in diameter. Form the bagels by making a ring and twisting the ends together to seal.

Preheat the oven to 375 degrees and bring 4 quarts of water to a boil. Add 2 tablespoons of brown sugar to the water. With a spatula, gently lower a few rings at a time into the boiling water, turning them after they rise to the surface and cooking an additional minute. Remove to a greased baking pan. Bake 25 to 30 minutes or until golden brown.

Robert Moses

ROBERT MOSES (1888–1981) was an urban planner who had tremendous influence on the city's landscape. He was park commissioner for over 25 years and also executive officer of the World's Fair Commission. In his role as park commissioner, Moses led the construction of hundreds of new playgrounds in New York City and was also responsible for building zoos, beaches, and housing. In 1934 alone, more than 1,700 Moses-led projects were completed.

Moses oversaw construction of more than 30 area highways, creating a parkway (no trucks) system spanning more than 400 miles, including the Grand Central Parkway in Queens and the Belt Parkway in Brooklyn. He pushed the creation of Flushing Meadow Park in northern Queens, filling in a swampy area of more than 1,200 acres formerly known as the Corona Dumps through the use of 6 million cubic yards of landfill, thus making it usable for the 1939 World's Fair.

Among other things, Moses was responsible for the construction of Shea Stadium, Lincoln Center, the Whitestone Bridge, Triborough Bridge, Throgs Neck Bridge, Verrazano-Narrows Bridge (the first bridge linking another part of the city to Staten Island), Queens Midtown Tunnel, and Brooklyn Battery Tunnel.

Some people today say Moses had too much power and changed the landscape too drastically; 250,000 people were displaced from their homes to make way for his projects. Others say he made great contributions to New York. But all agree that he was an influential figure who forever changed the city.

The United Nations

IN JUNE 1945, following the end of World War II, the United Nations (UN) Charter was signed in San Francisco, creating a permanent international peace organization.

The first UN session was held in March 1946 at Hunter College in the Bronx. Subsequently, the UN was headquartered at buildings on the World's Fair site and at Lake Success, in Nassau County.

The United Nations complex.

A permanent home was found when the millionaire John D. Rockefeller bought 17 acres of land along the East River between 42nd Street and 48th Street and donated it to the United Nations. The 510-foot-high Secretariat Building was completed in 1950, and the General Assembly Hall in 1952. Since its completion, the United Nations complex has hosted hundreds of important meetings.

Transportation Hub

During the early to mid-20th century, transatlantic ocean liners were the only way to cross the Atlantic. The best known ships were the British RMS *Queen Mary* (1936–1946) and *Queen Elizabeth* (1946–1969). They were a whopping 1,031 feet long, almost double the length of the largest 19th-century ships. When they sailed up the Hudson River, people took notice.

Beatlemania

The Beatles hit it big in their native England in 1963. By the end of January 1964, their song "I Want to Hold Your Hand" was at number one on the American pop charts. The group landed at Kennedy Airport on February 7, 1964, to a throng of 3,000 screaming fans, along with a huge contingent of reporters from all over the world. The Beatles made their first American television appearance on February 9 on *The Ed Sullivan Show*, recorded in midtown. CBS received 50,000 requests for tickets at a theater with 700 seats; 73 million people tuned in to watch the historic broadcast. They kicked off their American tour with a concert at Shea Stadium on August 15, 1965, in front of 55,000 fans. The screaming was so loud that it was almost impossible for anyone to hear any music. The Beatles returned to Shea on August 23, 1966.

After the Beatles broke up in 1970, John Lennon moved to New York with his wife, Yoko Ono. The pair lived in the Dakota apartment building at Central Park West and 72nd Street. On December 8, 1980, as he was returning home from a day of recording at the studio, Lennon was approached by a crazed fan and fatally shot. A crowd of 225,000 gathered in Central Park a few days later for 10 minutes of silence in Lennon's honor. A spot in the park called Strawberry Fields was created in his honor, and dedicated on October 9, 1985, on what would have been his 45th birthday.

Poster advertising New York's airports, 1936.

Ocean liners were eventually replaced by airplanes. The city's first airport was LaGuardia, built on the site of the Gala Amusement Park. In 1929, the park was transformed into a 105-acre private flying field and first named Glenn H. Curtiss Airport, after the aviation pioneer, and then renamed North Beach Airport. In 1937, the city took over and enlarged the airport, purchasing adjoining land and filling in 357 acres of waterfront. In 1939, it reopened with a new name: New York Municipal Airport–LaGuardia Field.

Another airport, Floyd Bennett Field, opened in 1930 in Brooklyn.

Then, in 1942, the city began placing fill over the marshy tidelands of Idlewild Golf Course in southern Queens to create a new airfield called Idlewild. Commercial flights began in 1948. The airport was renamed Kennedy in 1963, after the president's death. Kennedy Airport currently employs 35,000 people.

1970s New York

NEW YORK City in the mid-1970s was a city in crisis. Graffiti on the subways was out of control, and most subway cars were covered in it, both inside and out. The city's finances were also in bad shape.

The Yellow Cab

During the 1930s, strict licensing regulations were developed for New York City taxis to prevent having too many clogging the streets.

In 1967, the city ordered that all medallion taxi cabs be painted yellow, so New Yorkers knew which ones were licensed. Back then, the iconic taxis were made by the Checker Motor Company. More recent models have included the Chevy Caprice and the Ford Crown Victoria.

There are currently about 13,000 yellow taxis in New York City.

Yellow cabs fill the streets of New York.

In October 1975, one of the most famous headlines in New York City history was published in huge type on the front page of the *New York Post* after President Gerald Ford said that he would not approve federal aid to bail the city out of its financial crisis. FORD TO CITY: DROP DEAD it read.

Tourist attractions such as the Times Square District had lost their luster and were dirty and unpleasant. Then on July 13, 1977, a massive blackout caused by multiple lightning strikes plunged the city into darkness at 9:34 PM. Looting and vandalism of more than 2,000 stores followed, especially in parts of Brooklyn, Queens, and the Bronx. Thousands of looters and arsonists were arrested and over

400 police officers were injured in the mayhem. Though power was only out for a day, estimates of property losses ran as high as $1 billion.

On the positive side, the 110-story World Trade Center was completed in 1973, a symbol of New York's prestige.

The Javits Center.

The Rebirth

THE STAGNATION of the 1970s would not last long. During the 1980s, things began to turn around. For one, New York welcomed some new and notable buildings. In 1986, a sparkling new convention center opened, a crystal palace of steel and glass located between 34th and 38th Streets on 11th Avenue. Three and a half million people attend shows at the Javits Center every year. The 56-story Trump Tower, at Fifth Avenue and 56th Street, was completed in 1983.

Harlem experienced a resurgence, and its brownstones are today considered some of the city's finest. After his presidency, Bill Clinton opened an office on 125th Street in the center of Harlem.

The Marriott Marquis Hotel at 45th Street, completed in 1985, was the start of the Times Square revitalization, despite the fact that five historic theaters were demolished to make way for the new building. It is known for its glass elevators that soar up through an open courtyard more than 40 floors to a revolving rooftop restaurant.

By the 1990s, under Mayor Rudolph Giuliani, Times Square revitalization was in full swing. New restaurants and shops replaced seedy old establishments. Madame Tussaud's Wax Museum opened on 42nd Street in 2000.

The soaring New York Times Building opened in 2007 at Eighth Avenue and 40th Street. Including its mast, it is 1,046 feet high, one of the tallest buildings in the city. The lights on Broadway today are brighter and more colorful than ever.

9/11 and the Freedom Tower

TUESDAY MORNING, September 11, 2001, seemed to hold the promise of a beautiful late summer's day in New York City. The sky was blue, the weather fair, and people around the city were getting ready for work.

Within a few minutes, everything changed. At 8:46 AM, a plane that had been hijacked by terrorists slammed into the north tower of the World Trade Center. In the 16 minutes that followed, most New Yorkers thought it was some kind of horrible accident. A news helicopter raced to the scene, hovering near the gash in the building. Reporters speculated on what had happened.

Then, at 9:03 AM, another plane hit the south tower, and everyone knew the United States was under attack. Those trapped in the floors above the impact had no chance of survival. Fierce flames, fed by jet fuel, blocked their escape. Many placed frantic calls to their loved ones. Some jumped rather than die in the fire. Those below the impact floors raced down the crowded staircases as firemen and police raced up.

Before long there was another horror. Its structural integrity severely compromised, the south tower collapsed at 9:59 AM. The people left in the north tower had a half an hour more to escape before that building fell at 10:28. Chaos followed as survivors fled Ground Zero, as it became known. The official death toll of the World Trade Center attacks is 2,753.

One of the most moving sights in the days after the attacks was the countless handmade MISSING signs posted by friends and relatives of those who were known to have been at the Trade Center that morning. As the days passed, hope that survivors would be found vanished.

The healing process has been slow for many families, since remains of over 1,000 victims have still not been identified. A cloud of smoke and dust from the smoldering ruins lay over the site for weeks, visible from miles away. Many of the firefighters, rescue workers, and volunteers who worked at the site have since developed serious lung ailments.

A plan for developing Ground Zero was created, including a 1,776-foot-high Freedom Tower, easily the tallest building in New York, and a memorial to the victims on the original footprint of the Twin Towers.

The Freedom Tower under construction in 2012.

New York of the Future

NEW YORK's future is bright because past and present blend together so well. Vibrant neighborhoods such as Little Italy, Chinatown, Harlem, and Greenwich Village showcase the many different sides of New York.

The writer O. Henry once said about New York City, "It'll be a great place if they ever finish it."

But New York is a great place precisely because it is ever a work in progress, a dynamic and vital city.

New York City of the future, as imagined circa 1906.

Selected Bibliography

Berman, John S. *Central Park*. New York: Barnes & Noble, 2003.

Fodor's. *Around New York City with Kids*. 5th ed. New York: Fodor's, 2011.

Homberger, Eric. *The Historical Atlas of New York City: A Visual Celebration of 400 Years of New York City's History*. 2nd ed. New York: Henry Holt, 2005.

Jakobsen, Kathy. *My New York*. Anniversary ed. New York: Little, Brown Books for Young Readers, 2003.

Lowenstein, Alison. *City Kid New York: The Ultimate Guide for NYC Parents with Kids Ages 4–12*. New York: Universe Publishing, 2010.

Moscow, Henry. *The Street Book*. New York: Fordham University Press, 1990.

Panchyk, Richard. *Catholic New York City.* Charleston, SC: Arcadia Publishing, 2009.

Panchyk, Richard. *German New York City.* Charleston, SC: Arcadia Publishing, 2008.

Panchyk. *New York City Skyscrapers: A Postcard History.* Charleston, SC: Arcadia Publishing, 2010.

Sanderson, Eric W. *Mannahatta: A Natural History of New York City.* New York: Abrams, 2009.

Schoener, Allan. *New York: An Illustrated History of the People.* New York: W. W. Norton, 1998.

Schrafft, Nichole Wadsworth, and Peter Bennett. *A Field Guide to New York City.* Rockport, MA: Twin Lights Publishers, 2009.

Shumway, Floyd M. *Seaport City: New York in 1775.* New York: South Street Seaport Museum, 1975.

Sutherland, Cara A. *Bridges of New York City.* New York: Barnes & Noble, 2003.

White, Norval, Elliot Willensky, and Fran Leadon. *AIA Guide to New York City.* 5th ed. New York: Oxford University Press, 2010.

Places to Visit

Museum of the City of New York
1220 Fifth Avenue at 103rd Street
New York, NY 10029
(212) 534-1672
www.mcny.org
ALONG WITH the New-York Historical Society,
one of the two must-see places for the New York
City history buff.

The Tenement Museum
103 Orchard Street
New York, NY 10002
(212) 982-8420
www.tenement.org
THE MUSEUM features several researched and
restored tenement apartments.

New York City Fire Museum
278 Spring Street
New York, NY 10013
(212) 691-1303
http://nycfiremuseum.org/

New York City Police Museum
100 Old Slip
New York, NY 10005
(212) 480-3100
www.nycpolicemuseum.org

New-York Historical Society
170 Central Park West
New York, NY 10024
(212) 873-3400
www.nyhistory.org
Founded in 1804, it features an astonishing collection of artifacts from the city's history.

Ellis Island
(212) 363-3200
www.ellisisland.org
www.nps.gov/elis/index.htm

Statue of Liberty
Liberty Island
New York, NY 10004
(212) 363-3200
www.nps.gov/stli/index.htm

The Skyscraper Museum
39 Battery Place
New York, NY 10280
(212) 968-1961
www.skyscraper.org/home.htm

Museum of American Finance
48 Wall Street
New York, NY 10005
(212) 908-4110
www.moaf.org/index
Located in the heart of the financial district, this museum is a great place to learn more about New York's role in our country's finances.

National Museum of the American Indian
Alexander Hamilton US Custom House
One Bowling Green
New York, NY 10004
(212) 514-3700
www.nmai.si.edu
This museum is actually part of the Smithsonian. Visit also to see the interior of the imposing and historic Custom House building.

St. Patrick's Cathedral
14 East 51st Street
New York, NY 10022
(212) 753-2261
www.saintpatrickscathedral.org
One of New York's most famous sites, due in part to its central location.

Trinity Church
74 Trinity Place
New York, NY 10006
(212) 602-0800
www.trinitywallstreet.org
This Episcopal church is a 19th-century masterpiece, and the churchyard is full of old, historic graves. Also visit the nearby **St. Paul's Chapel**, built in 1766.

Index

Page numbers in *italics* indicate pictures